STAFF APPRAISAL IN SCHOOLS AND COLLEGES

A GUIDE TO IMPLEMENTATION

Editors: Brian Fidler and Robert Cooper

Longman

In association with
The British Educational Management
and Administration Society

Longman Group UK Limited
Longman House, Burnt Mill, Harlow, Essex, CM20 2JE

First published 1988

British Library Cataloguing in Publication Data

Staff appraisal in schools and colleges.
    1. Teachers——Great Britain——Rating of
    I. Fidler, Brian II. Cooper, Robert III. British Educational
    Management and Administration Association
    371.1'44'0941   LB2838

ISBN 0-582-02070-0

Printed and bound in Great Britain by
Biddles Ltd, Guildford and King's Lynn

CONTENTS

Preface

I am pleased to commend this book. It represents, in part, the product of two British Education Management Appraisal Conferences mounted in 1985 and 1986. The book distils the wisdom from these conferences and goes on to provide six case studies of appraisal as practised in primary and secondary schools and colleges.

Too often books on management issues can fail to draw on experience and developments across the various sectors in the education service. This book draws on experience in both schools and colleges to provide a helpful guide to the implementation and management of staff appraisal. It discusses the issues to be faced and the skills that have to be developed.

In the past two or three years I have found an increasing demand from teachers for someone to answer the question – 'How am I getting on? Am I performing well?' I have received complaints that people find themselves working in the dark. They may have visitors to the classroom who may or may not be passing judgement on their work and yet they are kept uninformed in the best traditions of 'mushroom management'. In contrast I have also readily responded to voluntary efforts to introduce appraisal. Quite recently I undertook a 'sample' appraisal interview with the head of a large secondary school in the presence of his senior staff because they are keen to get on and develop something for themselves. Appraisal should be a positive and supportive exercise aimed at raising morale and improving the effectiveness of the learning experience in schools and colleges. It is an essential element of school and college improvement.

This book is an essential aid to all those D.I.Y. experts who cannot wait for the seal of approval on national guidelines.

Derek Esp
Chair BEMAS
Director of Education
Lincolnshire

Acknowledgements

The inspiration for this book and much of the material was generated by two appraisal conferences which were put on by the Education Management Teachers' Committee of the British Educational Management and Administration Society in 1985 and 1986. The first conference studied appraisal experience in non-educational organisations and the second looked at developing practice in schools. We are grateful to the speakers and participants at those conferences for their contribution to our understanding of staff appraisal. In particular one of us (Brian Fidler) is indebted to one of the conference speakers, Nick Laycock of the Plant Protection Division of ICI, for an earlier talk at a 20 day school management course in which the positive attributes of staff appraisal and the organisational complexities of such a system were first made clear.

We wish to thank Len Watson, Roy McHugh and Mike Locke of BEMAS for their encouragement and support in this venture and Derek Esp, Chair of BEMAS, for contributing the preface.

The manuscript has been typed with great patience and breathtaking speed by Mrs Carole Butler and we have received word processing help from David Booth and Margaret Johnson. Finally we should like to thank the individual contributors to this volume who wrote and delivered their writings to a very demanding deadline. The success of this volume will be a reward for the high quality of their work.

Brian Fidler   Bob Cooper

July 1987.

The authors and publishers are grateful to the Further Education Staff College, Coombe Lodge, Blagdon, for permission to reproduce Appendixes A and B from A Staff Development Handbook in *Coombe Lodge Reports* (20).

Introduction

Brian Fidler and Bob Cooper

Context

Appraisal was mentioned in the Government White Paper 'Teaching Quality' in 1983 mainly as a device which would allow LEAs to build up data on the capabilities of their teachers. The word had scarcely been mentioned in educational circles before that date, although, as will be seen, some schools were already practising a form of staff appraisal. From such beginnings four years ago the situation has developed rapidly. In the 1986 Education Act (No.2) the Secretary of State took reserve powers which would allow him to impose an appraisal process by requiring local education authorities and others to ensure that the performance of teachers is regularly appraised in 'accordance with such requirement as may be prescribed'. Also in the draft conditions of service (DES 1987) which have been published recently there is a requirement to comply with an appraisal process 'within an agreed national framework'. Before making any regulations under the Act, the Secretary of State is required to consult LEA associations, representatives of teachers and others .Thus this book appears at a most opportune time.

Whilst it is clear that within a short time staff appraisal will be a regular feature of life in our schools and colleges, its exact form and purpose are still at a formative stage. Individual appraisal systems have been implemented in some schools and six LEAs (Croydon, Cumbria, Newcastle, Salford, Somerset and Suffolk) are conducting pilot studies with DES funding and more are also tentatively devising schemes. The results of these activities will be of great interest to those in schools, colleges and LEAs who are currently contemplating the introduction of some form of staff appraisal. Further guidance is available by studying practice in overseas educational systems which have a form of staff appraisal and, finally, there is the accumulated experience of operating staff appraisal in non-educational organisations – industry, commerce and other public services. It is the contention of this book that there is much to be learned from these sources which will be of great value to those for whom this book is written – *those in schools, colleges and LEAs who are about to implement, or will take part in, a process of staff appraisal*.

This is not simply a 'how to do it' book. The subject of staff appraisal is too complex and the context of individual schools and colleges is too varied to suggest that there is a 'right' way to design a staff appraisal system. It is for that reason that the book has theoretical and polemic sections. These are to aid understanding and challenge existing ideas. It is for each reader to think through his or her own design of an appraisal system. However, this book contains much stimulating material and much accumulated experience to aid this process. There is also much that is practical in this book. The implementation steps in the action plan provide a framework to guide practitioners in thinking through these detailed steps and provide a range of decisions to be made at each stage and illustrate the range of possibilities which may be considered before arriving at a decision.

This book particularly draws on the experience of six individual schools and colleges in England and Wales which have introduced a form of staff appraisal and also on the experience of non-educational organisations (mainly in the UK). These sources have been selected in order to present *a managerial approach to appraisal at the institutional level*. Much writing on appraisal has treated it as an issue in assessment; as a process which checks on the quality of teaching in a rather independent way. It would be possible in these terms to imagine 'professional' appraisers whose main task, either in addition to teaching or as a sole activity, would be to assess the teaching competence of staff in schools and colleges. Such judgements would then be passed on to others for action either in schools or in LEAs. Much American experience described in the Suffolk study (Suffolk Education Department 1985) is written from this perspective. Describing the results of an analysis of appraisal schemes in the USA in the late 1970s, Wood and Pohland (1983) found that the practice of teacher evaluation largely provided 'assessment suitable as a basis for administrative/organisational decision-making in the areas of staffing and compensation instead of ... efforts to improve teaching practices'. It is the contention of this book that industrial and other non-educational experience which sees appraisal as part of the managerial process of the institution offers a model which is positive and developmental and actually *could* lead to improvements in the education of children and young people. On the other hand, models which regard appraisal as synonymous with assessment are likely to prove politically unworkable, institutionally stultifying and lacking in technical validity.

The model propounded here accepts the inherent conflict of a process which is both evaluative and developmental and seeks to minimise such conflict. A managerial approach to appraisal is required because appraisal looks at the objectives and performance of individual members of staff. How such objectives and performance contribute to the overall work of the institution is a *vital* concern to the management of any organisation. Moreover, any proposals for further training or development which arise from an appraisal process require resources, human or financial, to make them possible, and deployment of resources is similarly a vital managerial concern. Finally appraisal provides an important opportunity for *two-way* communication between those who play a part in management and those who directly provide the service. However, let there be no misunderstanding, this is not to propose a particular *style of management.* Whilst all organisations have to be managed they do not have to be managed, in the same way. A highly participative collegial approach emphasising leadership and teamwork is one style of management. Further discussion of this theme is to be found in Section 1.2 and in Everard and Morris' book *Effective School Management* (1985). Other than advocating a managerial approach to staff appraisal within a school or college this book is not prescriptive and does not offer a blueprint for an appraisal system. Quite the reverse, it seeks to illustrate a diversity of opinion and practice. However, on reading through the case-studies and theoretical writings the reader will observe a number of common threads. These are brought together in the final section of the book. In the early sections of the book and elsewhere much use is made of the noun *organisation.* This is not used in an especially technical sense but rather because of its generality and consequent economy of writing. It can be taken to mean any group of people working together for a purpose. As such it then covers a commercial firm, an industrial factory, the civil service, a school, college or LEA. A more detailed illustration of the concept is given by Paisey (1981).

The structure of the book

This book is somewhat more than an edited collection of individual contributions. It has substantial sections written by the editors which facilitate continuity by providing an analytical framework for other contributions, a consideration of management implications of appraisal, and a concluding discussion and action plan. It is one of the first books to make a detailed study of an aspect of school management – other collections have tried to cover the whole of school management in one volume. Such is the increase in sophistication of the study of school management that this is no longer credible for all but the most summary treatments.

The book begins with a theoretical discussion of the rationale for appraisal in general terms and an exploration of the problems associated with the process in any organisation with some suggested solutions. Reference is made to the pervasive influence of the **management by objectives approach** leading to concentration on key result areas and target-setting. Some particular difficulties associated with adapting a managerial approach to appraisal in schools and colleges are outlined and assessed. From this section a set of criteria is devised which an appraisal system should meet.

The second section juxtaposes two seemingly different proposals for an appraisal system in schools. David Trethowan advocates a target-setting approach whilst David Styan proposes a less managerial and more collegial approach. Both, however, see improved performance of staff as the outcome and both see that as being achieved by growth and development and not by coercion. Also in this section Joan Dean identifies the ways in which a local authority will be required to support and co-ordinate appraisal in its institutions and ensure comparable standards are being achieved. When considering the developmental opportunities which may be identified in the appraisal interview of an individual in an institution it is clear that courses of training or work experience in another school or college will require co-ordination across more units than an individual institution and this is clearly an appropriate level of activity for an LEA.

The third section contains a short summary of appraisal activity in education followed by the major part of this section which is six case studies of appraisal in action. There are two each from primary and secondary schools, plus one each from a tertiary college and a further education college. These case-studies reflect the particular strategies and approach used in each institution. They were chosen to reflect diversity of practice although there are striking similarities in both implementation strategies and the approach to appraisal which was adopted. It should be made clear that these six make no claim to be representative nor would they wish to claim that their practice was exemplary; but it is clear from reading the case-studies that they illustrate good practice.

Section 4 brings together a series of issues and skills which are important in implementing an appraisal system in a school or college. Ray Sumner studies the conceptual and practical difficulties of assessing teaching performance and offers a matrix of some 18-22 ways which could be used to contribute to an overall assessment. Bob Cooper and John West-Burnham have written a chapter which examines some of the management implications of implementing an appraisal scheme in a school or college.

Two types of interview skills are considered. Keith Diffey draws out the skills needed for effective appraisal interviewing in a problem-solving mode whilst Stephen Chelms looks at the related skills which are required in counselling interviews.

Finally in this section Alan and Audrey Paisey present some training exercises which could be used by groups of teachers or whole school and college staffs to stimulate discussion about appraisal and the readiness of the organisation for appraisal.

The final section of the book contains a summary and an action plan. The action plan provides a framework to plan the introduction of an appraisal system and illustrates the range of decisions which have to be made at each stage.

The book is intended to be self-contained although those who require further details, and students on courses in education management, will find a very full set of references which they may follow up.

We doubt that anyone will read this book from cover to cover sequentially. We envisage that readers will first dip into it according to their state of knowledge and attitude to appraisal. We suggest that those who know little about appraisal or are sceptical of the process should first read the case studies in Section 3. We think they will find there much that is reassuring and heartening. We think that readers will find much value in also reading the case-studies from sectors other than the one in which they teach.

Those who know more and wish to organise their thoughts might start at Section 1 or Section 2.

Before moving to develop and implement an appraisal system all readers would be advised to read Sections 1 and 4 before Sections 2, 3 and 5.

Aims of staff appraisal

We propose three requirements for an appraisal system:

1. It should carry credibility with the public as a check on the quality of work in schools and colleges.

2. It should lead to improvements in the learning experiences of pupils and students.

3. It should lead to greater job satisfaction of all those who work in schools and colleges.

We believe that these are difficult and, professionally, very challenging aims but that no worthwhile appraisal system should ignore any of them. Any appraisal system should work progressively towards meeting all three more fully. These are summary aims within which we believe all other objectives can be subsumed.

We hope as a result of reading this book readers may be enabled to look at the concept of appraisal differently because of the insights they have acquired.

To begin to work towards the aims above it is important for all those who work in the education service to understand the appraisal process so that they can play their part and benefit. This is just as true for those who are to be appraised as for those who are to do the appraising. However, we must make clear our fundamental belief that the quality of the appraisal process can only be as good as the skills of the managers who play such a key part in the whole process.

SECTION 1
CONCEPTS AND
APPLICATIONS IN
NON-EDUCATIONAL
ORGANISATIONS

1.1   Theory, Concepts and Experience in Other Organisations

Brian Fidler

Introduction

Much of the writing on appraisal by educationalists has more of the flavour of accountability, assessment and evaluation about it than is the current practice in other organisations. It is possible that this reflects a stereotypical view of the assumed authoritarian style used by managers in industry and commerce. Whereas in fact what is quite striking, when looking at the theory of appraisal and its practice in well-managed industry, commerce and other public services, is that appraisal is quite positive and developmental. Many of the anticipated problems of applying appraisal to educational situations have also been experienced in other organisations and there is a great deal that can be learned from their experience which will enable managers in education to avoid the same mistakes. Unless we study and learn from the experience of others we shall find ourselves with either a cosy system which achieves little and lacks public credibility, or a system which is Draconian in its application and similarly achieves little because of the hostile reaction it provokes. Almost all of the concepts of appraisal in other organisations can be taken over into an educational context. The one feature which may have no parallel in other organisations is any requirement to observe systematically the work performance of the appraisee. Thus there appears to be no equivalent of observation of teaching performance.

This section describes the theory of appraisal and identifies inherent conflicts in the process. It briefly examines experience in other organisations. Section 1.2 looks at a number of problems associated with translating such experience to schools and colleges. Finally, a checklist of essential features of an appraisal system is produced which acts as a summary of this section.

Terms

Staff appraisal is the term used in this book for the process by which an employee and his or her superordinate meet to discuss the work performance of the employee. There is a huge variety of terms used – performance appraisal, performance review, performance evaluation, staff review, staff reporting and more especially teacher appraisal, teacher assessment – which have no accepted difference of meaning. Staff development, on the other hand, as the name implies, is wholly concerned with the increase of knowledge, skill or experience of staff without the evaluative connotation associated with appraisal.

Increasingly, however, staff appraisal has been concerned with staff development. Recently staff appraisal has concentrated on improving individual performance at work and so the two terms have become closer.

Another related process is institutional evaluation. Inevitably school and college evaluation reflect on an individual teacher's performance and in many schemes of institutional review there are self-appraisal or self-review documents for staff to complete. However, in this book the focus is upon staff appraisal as a managerial activity whereby a manager engages in an appraisal process with a subordinate for whom he or she is, in some sense, accountable.

Appraisal system and interview

It is helpful to differentiate between the appraisal interview and the whole system of which it is a part. The system comprises all the papers and procedures involved in appraisal.

Accountability and development

The GRIDS handbooks (McMahon et al 1984) envisage self-review of individual teachers for internal development purposes as leading to a staff development programme, whilst if the focus were on formal external accountability then this would lead to a staff appraisal scheme. This implies a neat conceptualisation which identifies appraisal with accountability but not with development. As we shall see (p.6) in non-educational organisations, appraisal is concerned with both individual development and accountability or evaluation and it is precisely this combination which gives appraisal such central importance and which also makes it so difficult to accomplish.

In designing a particular appraisal system it is important to be quite clear about the extent to which it is intended to be evaluative and the extent to which it should lead to individual development. It may be useful conceptually to try to mark the position of a particular system on a display which has evaluation and development as axes (Figure 1). An appraisal system could be placed anywhere between the axes depending on its particular balance between evaluation and development.

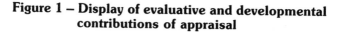

Increasing evaluative concern

X   a pay review   X   an appraisal system

X   A staff development programme

Increasing developmental concern

Figure 1 – Display of evaluative and developmental contributions of appraisal

We shall later return to the fundamental contradictions inherent in using appraisal for both evaluative and developmental functions.

Appraisal theory

Appraisal of some kind has been used in organisations for a long time. In industrial and commercial concerns it was initially used in the 1920s to assess workers' rewards. Although the process became more sophisticated, it was basically used as a performance control strategy in a rather mechanical way. Much effort was devoted to developing rating scales of personal qualities of workers.

After World War II three different types of appraisal could be distinguished:

      (a)   reward review;
      (b)   performance review;
      (c)   review of potential for promotion.

As we shall see there may be inherent conflicts in these three types of activity.

The theory of appraisal really came of age with the advent of the Management by Objectives (MBO) movement in the 1960s.

Management by Objectives

Although the concept is generally attributed to Peter Drucker, it was Douglas McGregor who allied it to performance appraisal (Strauss 1972). MBO is seen by many as a device for ensuring that employees in an organisation are all engaged on work which is consistent with the organisation's overall objectives as identified by the most senior personnel in the organisation. Others have seen MBO as emphasising employee participation, better communication and enhanced motivation through clearly identified goals and the achievement of results (Giegold 1978).

Schuster and Kindall (1974) have identified three structural elements to MBO:

1.   Performance goals or targets initiated periodically by the employee.

2.   Mutual agreement on a set of goals by the employee and his
     superior after discussion.

3.   Periodic review by the employee and his superior of the match
     between goals and achievements.

These are the features of MBO which changed the nature of the
appraisal process. The appraisal process is then concerned with the
performance of employees as demonstrated by the extent to which
they have achieved targets to which they were committed. Some
appraisal systems use MBO explicitly whilst others concentrate on
performance and may talk about targets and results without taking on
all the features of an MBO approach. Clearly an appraisal interview
has a very clear rationale under MBO and so this approach has been
very pervasive.

Appraisal and management

Whether appraisal is on classical lines or part of MBO it is quite clear as
Freemantle (1985) says in **Superboss**, that 'appraisal is an integral
part of management, not a system external to it'. Beer (1986) also
points out 'performance evaluation is an important element in the
information and control system of most complex organisations'.
Appraisal has implications for the appraisee, the appraiser, central
planning and control of the organisation, and the outside world. It is an
all-embracing process. Since generally there is a concentration of
attention on the appraisee and appraiser, it is worthwhile to state the
range of purposes which appraisal may serve for central planning and
control of an organisation. Stewart and Stewart (1977) list the
following:
    (a)   manpower skills audit;
    (b)   manpower forecasting;
    (c)   assessment of employee potential;
    (d)   succession planning;
    (e)   salary planning;
    (f)   training planning;
    (g)   equity between subordinates;
    (h)   downward transmission of company objectives;
    (i)   problem and grievance detection and handling.
For a public service organisation accountability to the outside world is
also an important purpose of an appraisal system.

Goals of performance appraisal

In an excellent recent review article, Beer (1986) has identified the main theoretical issues in performance appraisal.

(i)   *For the manager (and the organisation)*

In addition to providing data to the central planning and control function in the organisation, appraisal is of direct benefit to the manager. It is a 'major tool for changing individual behaviour' (Beer 1986). The goals cover both evaluation and development. Beer lists eight:

1.   evaluation goals
     (a)   To give feedback to subordinates so they know where they stand.
     (b)   To develop valid data for pay and promotion decisions and to aid communication of these.
     (c)   To provide a means of warning subordinates about unsatisfactory performance.
2.   development goals
     (a)   To counsel and coach subordinates so that they will improve their performance and develop future potential.
     (b)   To develop commitment to the organisation through discussion of career opportunities and career planning.
     (c)   To motivate subordinates through recognition of achievements and support.
     (d)   To strengthen supervisor-subordinate relations.
     (e)   To diagnose individual and organisational problems.

Categorising these goals as evaluation or development emphasises that some of them are in conflict. The appraisal relationship required for the evaluation goals will be inimical to the trusting open relationship required for development. It is important for appraisal systems to recognise this problem. Decisions on pay and promotability can be separated in time from more developmental activities whilst within the appraisal interview there may be a sequencing of activities which seeks to minimise the potential conflict (see p.10).

(ii)   *For the individual employee*

Individuals have a number of possible goals which they may achieve by taking part in appraisal. Six major benefits can be identified.

1. To receive feedback on their performance and progress.
2. To discuss their present job and amend their job description if changes are agreed.
3. To identify opportunities for professional personal development.
4. To identify training opportunities.
5. To discuss their aspirations and career plans.
6. To discuss problems in the organisation and their relationship with their manager.

When feedback is positive and is consistent with the employee's own self image, the inherent conflicts in the process are minimised; however, when the feedback is critical of poor performance, a defensive reaction from an employee may set up barriers which inhibit acceptance of this feedback and prevent open discussion of how performance might be improved.

Beer (1986) identifies the most fundamental conflict as that between the individual and the organisation.

'The individual desires to confirm a positive self image and to obtain organisational rewards of promotion or pay. The organisation wants individuals to be open to negative information about themselves so that they can improve their performance. As long as individuals see the appraisal process as having an important influence on their rewards (pay, recognition), their career (promotions and reputation), and their self image they will be reluctant to engage in the kind of open dialogue required for valid evaluation and personal development.' (p.289)

Clearly this conflict is at its most acute when dealing with poor performers. Inevitably an appraisal system which covers all employees will throw up a small minority whose performance is below an acceptable standard. This is known to happen in all organisations and there is a great temptation to avoid the issue by both parties in the name of good relations. This is at best a paliative and at worst undermines the whole appraisal system and leads to no improvement for the individual. This is a problem to which we shall return (p.10).

Reducing the fundamental conflict

Beer identifies a number of measures which tend to lessen the fundamental conflict.

(i)   *Separating evaluation and development*

As far as possible these purposes should be separated. Any concern with pay or promotion should be removed from the main developmental appraisal process. Separating these purposes in time by six months is often suggested.

(ii)   *Choosing appropriate performance data*

Performance data has to be related to the job being done. A systematic approach to this (Stenning and Stenning 1984) requires

(a)   A clear comprehensive and accurate job description.
(b)   A statement of the results expected of the job holder which are as objective and measurable as possible.
(c)   A clear description of the abilities, skills, knowledge and personal characteristics of effective job performers.
(d)   Data systematically assembled over the review period.

A comprehensive approach would suggest that each element of a job description should have an associated standard of performance attached to it. However, this approach suffers from two major disadvantages. One is that job descriptions typically have a large number of individual tasks and each of these would require a standard of performance. The second problem is that a multi-element job description provides no indication of the priority which should be attached to each individual element

The MBO approach is to select a limited number of important parts of the job description and to designate these 'key result areas' (Morrisey 1976). These five to 10 specific areas then have objectives or measurable results associated with them. In addition to these work objectives which ensure the efficient operation of the organisation, there would be personal development objectives which were intended to ensure growth and development of the individual (in areas not incompatible with organisational objectives).

An alternative approach suggested by Odiorne (Morrisey 1983) where much of the work is on going and repetitive is to identify three levels of objectives. The basic level of **regular or routine objectives** assumes that there are already well established levels of performance for most of an individual's work activities. To deal with problems which have been identified in the routine work there would then be **problem-solving objectives**. Finally there would be **innovative objectives** which represent a major change or development in the work of an individual which would benefit the organisation. The personal development objectives could involve both problem-solving and innovation. This latter approach may be worthy of consideration in trying to appraise the work of teachers.

The appraisal interview provides an opportunity to review periodically the job description and to amend it to ensure that it is a faithful record of the current job.

Clarity can be achieved and defensiveness minimised if feedback on performance refers to specific behaviours and actual incidents as exemplars of more general behaviour. This data, however, must be collected over a substantial period and not only refer to incidents in the preceding week or two otherwise it will lack credibility in the eyes of the appraisee.

On the other hand any problems should be discussed with the employee as they happen and not stored up only to be discussed at the appraisal interview. Supervision and coaching should be continuous, as should any modification of targets and objectives arising from new circumstances. The appraisal interview should summarise and recap such events during the year – not add new evidence.

Whilst an MBO approach focuses on accomplishments which are tangible, it is less concerned with how they are achieved and there may have been organisational reasons which precluded success and are no reflection on the performance of the appraisee. It is suggested that behavioural ratings on the way objectives were achieved should supplement the MBO performance data as these would be useful for development purposes.

(iii)   *Recognising individual differences in system designs*

Beer suggests that not all employees should be appraised with the same frequency. Some, particularly the upwardly mobile, may need more feedback on performance whilst those who are competent but have reached the peak of their capabilities should only be appraised every two or three years.

(iv)   *Upward appraisal*

Allowing an employee to rate the performance of his or her manager can help to break down barriers and may give the manager useful feedback on how his or her performance is perceived. It can generate a dialogue and allow the manager to demonstrate the open non-defensive behaviour which it is hoped the employee may also show.

(v)   *Using an appropriate interview style*

Maier (1976) has characterised three interview styles as *'Tell and Sell'*, *'Tell and Listen'* and *'Problem-Solving'*. These may be appropriate for different interview situations. In the 'Tell and Sell' method, the manager directs the interview and gains the acceptance of the appraisee to take steps to improve performance. The 'Tell and Listen' style requires the manager to give authentic feedback but then to allow the appraisee to respond. Communication and understanding may be much improved. Changes in performance, however, depend upon a change of attitude following improved communication.

The 'Problem-Solving' style as the name implies requires both appraiser and appraisee jointly to acknowledge problems and to work on them together.

Beer suggests that a mixed-mode interview moving from the 'Problem-Solving' style to the 'Tell and Sell' or 'Tell and Listen' may be appropriate for a variety of situations. This would permit open-ended discussion of problems and possible solutions before moving to an agreed plan, but would also allow the manager to ensure that difficult issues are faced if they are not raised by the appraisee.

Other research evidence suggests that agreeing the content and process of the appraisal interview beforehand is worthwhile. Self-appraisal by the employee in preparation for the interview allows for a more equal discussion in the interview and provides an opportunity for the appraisee to prepare any problems which he or she wishes to raise about the job, the organisation, or their relationship with their manager. The interview should conclude with a concrete plan for performance improvement. Such a plan should encompass any training required and any new aspects of the job which are to provide development. Clearly it is vital that any training, job change or other resource which is agreed upon is actually provided. Cynicism can be expected fairly rapidly if commitments on one side are not met.

Management and poor performance

A point worth emphasising is that the appraisal interview is the one formal occasion in the year when employee and manager sit down to discuss work performances; but there should be informal on-going discussions particularly if improvement needs guiding and monitoring. The appraisal interview may need supplementing with a counselling interview either if intensive help is needed or a neutral exploration of issues is required. For cases of extreme and persistent underperformance, a separate disciplinary interview may be required.

Steinmetz (1985) has presented a useful analysis of reasons for unsatisfactory performance. These are characterised as:
  (a) managerial or organisational shortcomings,
  (b) individual personal shortcomings of the employee, and
  (c) outside influences.

Cutting across these, however, is the fundamental attitude of the employee to the job (see Figure 2).

In addition to the suggestions of Steinmetz written from US experience, the book by Stewart and Stewart (1983) **Managing the Poor Performer**, offers some constructive advice for improving performance based on UK experience starting from the premise 'nobody should be identified as a poor performer without his being told'. They provide a useful description of various facets of poor performance to aid the recognition of poor performance and also a valuable checklist of questions for managers to ask of themselves in order to confirm their initial judgement of poor performance. A rather more pessimistic assessment of US experience of improving teacher competence is provided by Bridges (1986) in **The Incompetent Teacher**. He finds some evidence of improvement in the performance of younger teachers but concludes, 'those who maintain that remediation is the way to solve the problem of teacher competence will not discover much support for their view in this book'.

Reason for failure	Whose problem	Remarks
Can't do	Management	1. Training 2. Provide resources 3. Remove obstacles
Won't do	Individual	Change Attitude
Doesn't know what he/she should be doing	Management	Improve communication

Figure 2 – The causes and correction of performance failure
[adapted from Steinmetz (1985)]

In his small-scale study of mainly secondary schools in the UK, Everard (1986a) reported that 'few schools reported no serious problems of inadequate staff performance', and more worryingly, 'the relatively few there are have an influence on the head's peace of mind and the school's reputation out of all proportion to their numbers'. Appraisal procedures will throw up evidence of poor performance. Some shortcomings in otherwise good performance can be tackled by setting targets which raise these particular aspects of performance to acceptable standards. More serious evidence of under-performance might best be tackled by more intensive coaching and counselling outside of normal appraisal procedures. The procedures developed by Montgomery (1984) may be helpful in this respect (see p.131). And only where such positive and developmental efforts are ineffective should separate disciplinary procedures be instigated.

Keeping efforts to improve poor performers separate from normal appraisal procedures will help prevent the impression being created that appraisal is concerned primarily with removing incompetent teachers. There is a real danger of this because the time spent on poor performers will be disproportionately greater than for other staff and could be seen, therefore, as the real thrust of the appraisal system. Whereas the real thrust should be the improvement of the performance of *all* staff.

Organisational culture

The final point is that the appraisal system must be consistent with the organisational culture. If the organisation is participative, dynamic, and has a clear sense of direction, then the appraisal system should reflect this by following a target-setting, problem-solving approach. If, however, the organisation is more authoritarian and hierarchical, then the appraisal system should mirror this more evaluative approach. Mixed messages are more likely to be confusing than successful. As Long (1986) reported after studying 300 appraisal systems '"ready made" systems imported from other organisations rarely function satisfactorily, partly because of organisational cultural differences'.

Experience of appraisal in non-educational organisations

Fletcher and Williams (1985) in their book *Performance Appraisal and Career Development* describe the history of appraisal practice and give an 'Identikit picture' of a British appraisal system. They look at problems and issues encountered in operating appraisal systems and also try to foresee future developments.

A feature of appraisal systems is that they are constantly being changed and reviewed. Long (1986) found that one third of the systems in his survey had been in operation for three years or less. It is, therefore, somewhat difficult to describe adequately this moving picture. However, from two recent surveys by the Institute of Personnel Managers in 1977 and 1986 some trends are clear (Gill 1977; Long 1986).

Purpose of appraisal

In each sample of around 300 organisations, over 80% had performance appraisal systems and very few had abandoned appraisal. *By 1986 most systems were primarily concerned with improving current performance rather than future potential.* Other important purposes were to set performance objectives and to assess training and development needs. Although not directly using MBO, almost two thirds of schemes used a results-oriented approach to appraisal.

Appraisal documents

Appraisal forms generally consisted of a combination of rating scales and open-ended questions. Fletcher and Williams (1985) describe a typical appraisal form as having four sides. The first has biographical details of the job holder and a job description. The final page, which is not generally seen by the job holder, has an assessment of the job holder's promotability and long-term potential. Whereas all previous sections are completed by the appraiser, this page has a section for the manager's manager to comment. The middle two pages written by the manager list the objectives which the appraisee has been concentrating on in the past year and comments on the extent to which these have been achieved. The manager outlines possible future improvements in performance and associated training and development needs. The manager gives an overall performance rating typically on a seven-point scale from 'poor' to 'outstanding'.

There is a space at this point for the appraisee to sign the report and to add any comments which he or she wishes (knowing that these will be read by the manager's manager). However, Long reported that only half the organisations had a formal appeals mechanism.

Interview

Over 80% of organisations had an interview preparation form for appraisees. The interview was reported to be generally problem-oriented with a joint problem-solving style of operation rather than being evaluative and judgemental. Almost all organisations provided notes of guidance for appraisees and almost 80% provided appraisal interview training. The practice of combining reviews of performance and potential has declined in the later survey.

Main weaknesses reported

There were three main weaknesses reported by Long's survey respondents.

1.   Unequal standards of assessment amongst different appraisers.

2.   Some lack of commitment to the process among line managers.

3.   Some lack of follow-up action on training and development plans.

There was growing recognition that a successful appraisal system has to attempt to meet the needs of individuals, line managers and the organisation.

Some particular systems

Fletcher and Williams (1985) provide (anonymous) case studies of appraisal systems in a variety of organisations. The Civil Service has published a trainer's resource pack (1985) which both describes its system and prepares appraisers and appraisees to use the system. It contains a training manual, a video and an audio tape (available from CFL Vision, Chalfont Grove, Gerrards Cross, Bucks SL9 8TN). This marks a major change of emphasis in the Civil Service appraisal system towards improvement of current performance and uses a results-oriented approach. This is a major attempt by a non-profit making service organisation to use this approach.
The appraisal system at the Plant Protection Division of ICI is described in the proceedings of a BEMAS appraisal conference

(Laycock 1987). This division of ICI employs a large number of professional scientists engaged in research and development work. Although part of a commercial organisation, this particular division has the problem of professionals engaged in work where it is not easy to assess results, and particularly where some of them may be very long term. The Civil Service and this division of ICI appear to offer closer parallels to the situation in educational organisations than most other industrial and commercial organisations.

Other appraisal experience is described by Everard (1986b) and Hayes (1984). Everard mainly describes experience at ICI, whilst Hayes chronicles the introduction of appraisal at Nicholas International. The Suffolk study (1985) describes some general industrial and commercial experience. Richardson (1987), writing from an industrial perspective, examines the training and development policies of large multinational companies and considers their applicability to a 'mass public service profession' such as education.

In a recent article Whyte (1986) surveys some management literature on appraisal mainly between 1980 and 1984 to look for implications for teacher appraisal. The article interposes US and British non-educational appraisal practice and has a section which deals with possible gender bias in appraisal.

1.2 Problems of Adaptation to Education

Brian Fidler

Introduction

When studying the theory of appraisal and its application in other organisations it is clear that there are substantial differences in the context and climate compared to publicly funded educational institutions. I have identified seven problem areas which are discussed here, concerned with adapting this experience to schools and colleges and suggest some ways forward. Two particular issues arising which are further explored are the nature of 'line management' in education and the appraisal of heads of institution. Finally, I list the features of an appraisal scheme which seem to be most important from the foregoing theory and experience.

Problem areas

(i)   *Management of professionals*

The management of professionals poses a basic problem. Handy (1984) describes many professionals as independent operators and in this model, management and appraisal are inappropriate. However, as organisations become more complex, co-ordination of some kind is required and for larger organisations some form of management is essential, particularly in turbulent times. With the gradual acceptance of management in education, a balance has to be struck between management approaches and professionalism. This is a situation met in some other spheres where appraisal is used.

(ii)   *Results unclear*

When the purpose of the whole organisation is somewhat unclear, then appraisal of the leader is particularly problematic and this is also true of others in the organisation. The problem of assessing institutional performance is in three parts: the first is to decide on the purposes or objectives of the institution. These are generally many and complex. The second is to find ways of assessing how well those objectives have been met. Some may be assessed quantitatively but most can only be assessed qualitatively. The third is how to make valid comparisons between institutions when the nature of the output in terms of educated students is crucially dependent on the level of ability and other characteristics of the students on entry, and over which the school or college has little direct control. Even at the level of examination performance comparisons between schools can be radically transformed when adjustments are made for the quality of the intake (Gray 1982). This is also the case when the results of an individual school are compared over time (Glogg 1986). Such adjustments can be done in a quantitative way for exam results. How much more difficult then to make such adjustments conceptually for those measures of output which can only be assessed qualitatively. For a discussion of recent research on school effectiveness see Reynolds (1985). Finally, when the success of the institution can be assessed, there is a further problem associated with assessing the contribution of the leader to that success.

Institutions need to be clear about their purpose even if the purpose may be difficult to assess except in qualitative terms. A statement of objectives provides the yardstick against which to assess performance. All other organisations have a multiplicity of objectives and need internal performance measures. Many of these are difficult to assess. Commercial firms have other objectives in addition to overall profitability.

(iii)   *Rewards uncertain*

Industrial and commercial organisations generally have rewards which they are able to bestow after assessing work performance. Thus financial and other benefits are connected with appraisal. The connection may not be direct – it may be staggered in time – but there is a relationship. There is no way in educational practice of directly rewarding good work in any financial sense. Sir Keith Joseph, one of the most fervent disciples of relating payment and performance, came to accept that merit pay or annual increments should not be related to annual appraisal procedures (DES 1986). Although there are no such annual merit awards in education, data collected through appraisal could be reflected in references and promotion some time in the future. However, personal and professional recognition of achievement should not be underestimated in its motivating potential.

(iv)   *Difficulty of assessing teaching*

Assessing the work of a teacher is particularly difficult. There are no universally agreed criteria for good teaching and more fundamentally the relationship between teaching and learning is not direct. Further discussion of these issues is continued in Section 4.1. It may well be that assessing teaching performance, let alone pupil learning, may not be defensible in any research sense but if it is part of a management process then the test to be applied to the assessment is one of 'fitness for purpose'. It is then important to decide on realistic standards of performance. As Ray Sumner observes in Section 4.1, 'the utility of taking an ideal as the standard for judging performance seems highly questionable'. Yet that is what tends to happen when describing teaching performance. A counsel of perfection is not an adequate baseline for judgment. If a realistic standard of competent performance on various aspects of the teacher's job can be agreed, then the assessment of teaching performance might reduce to an overall acceptable/unacceptable judgement. Remedial measures will be needed for those judged unacceptable whilst for the overwhelming majority who are judged acceptable there may be individual elements of performance which need raising in standard and which could be set as targets for the coming year. For the **acceptable** the dialogue between appraiser and appraisee would be a professional dialogue intended to stimulate reflection and new ideas. A danger of a checklist approach to assessing teaching performance as observed by Peaker (1986) after a visit to the USA, is that it tends to encourage 'safe' teaching, i.e. static and didactic teaching. Whilst measuring the work of teaching presents problems, so does measuring the work performance of intermediate level personnel in other organisations and particularly those in service functions within the organisation.
No other organisation observes the work performance of its personnel in ways which resemble classroom observation.

(v)   *Too many bosses*

For headteachers and most teachers in secondary schools there is no direct superordinate. The head has a number of people and groups to whom he or she is accountable. Equally, those in secondary schools with both subject and pastoral duties have at least two people to whom they are accountable. This more complicated form of organisation is usually referred to as a matrix structure and has been more usually associated with further and higher education (Fidler 1984). The pastoral-academic matrix organisation of the secondary school does have counterparts in other organisations (Morrisey 1983), but generally there is a strong arm of the matrix which is close to line management and through which the major elements of appraisal proceed. Problems of co-ordination and communication between the two people to whom an individual is accountable have been noted. Schools will need to consider such problems and ensure that data on performance in other tasks is fed into a designated main appraisal chain.

(vi)   *Lack of time*

Appraisal carried out properly in any organisation takes a lot of time. This poses acute problems in education where generally the time allowed for management is too small (Handy 1984). Other organisations accept the importance of appraisal and regard the time taken by the process as an efficient use of time. In education a combination of . not giving a full appraisal to every teacher every year and finding extra management time to carry out appraisal will have to be used to tackle the time problem.

Various estimates of the time required for appraisal have been made. The second Suffolk report (Suffolk Education Department 1987) assumed that an appraisee would appraise only seven teachers and involve three periods of classroom observation for each of them. This would take 5.25 hours for each teacher. In addition there would be initial and on-going time required for training in appraisal skills. There would also be a need for extra administrative and clerical staff. The costs are assessed at £125 per teacher and £600-£1,100 per headteacher.

(vii)   *Lack of infrastructure in LEAs*

Well managed organisations recognise that there are service functions which need to be provided to those carrying out the direct work of the organisation. Two of these directly link with appraisal – personnel and training. Personnel oversees the whole process of appraisal and co-ordinates such work across the organisation. It ensures that action is taken as a result of appraisal, be this training, a job change, career progression, or whatever. Training looks at training needs across the organisation and either provides or purchases training to meet these needs. Whilst some aspects of both these may be carried out at school level by a professional tutor type appointment, there is a need for both these functions to be co-ordinated right across an LEA. This would provide a unit of ample size and scope for both these functions to be carried out effectively and efficiently. But this will pose new manpower needs for every LEA.

Appraisal and line managers

In other organisations line managers play a key role in the appraisal process because appraisal is an integral part of the management process not an unrelated activity.

It is line managers who control and direct the activity of subordinates, are accountable for their performance and control resources which may support and improve their performance. These activities go on throughout the year and an appraisal interview is the formal stage in the year for taking stock of these activities.

Although the term *line manager* may conjure up the vision of an authoritarian figure barking out orders, the term also applies to a leader operating within a team in a participative, problem-solving mode. The term here is used to identify the person who is accountable for the operation of a section of the organisation and who has human and other resources available to achieve results. It is a matter of style how the manager operates in order to achieve these results. In an organisation largely staffed by professionals the successful approach is more likely to involve leadership and teamwork than a bureaucratic authoritarian style.

However, from the point of view of accountability and control of resources, the team leader has the attributes of a line manager and this is the term other organisations use. If this term jars, then the reader should replace it with the term *team leader* when thinking about appraisal in education.

Line managers in education

In educational institutions the identification of a line manager has hardly been considered. In a primary school it is clear that the head-teacher occupies a position equivalent to a line manager from the point of view of a teacher within the school, although where there are team leaders they may exercise a middle management role. In a secondary school, on the other hand, the position is much less clear. First, in a typical secondary school, there are too many teachers for the headteacher to exercise a direct line management function. Second, there are two sets of middle managers in the pastoral-academic matrix structure as has already been remarked. The most stable grouping is the academic or subject grouping and so this is probably the most appropriate to identify with line management-type functions. It may be that if heads of department are required to appraise staff within their department, this will bring about a more managerial outlook from such middle managers (see also p.137). As line managers these middle managers are both appraised and also appraise others. The main thrust of the appraisal of this group should probably concentrate on their managerial function rather than their classroom performance since their key role is to manage their departments or pastoral teams and thereby contribute to the overall work of the school. However, their teaching performance should not be neglected. Appraisals should be carried out by this group of middle managers before they themselves are appraised since the appraisal reports which they write provide information on their management performance. This is the sequencing of appraisals practised at ICI (Laycock 1987).

Colleges with a matrix structure will similarly have to identify middle managers who are to carry the main appraisal function.

Heads of institutions

Other organisations have most difficulty in appraising senior management. In the case of educational organisations, difficulties are compounded by the fact that heads of institutions do not have an equivalent of a line manager. Legally they are accountable to their governing bodies and in employment terms they are employed by a local authority which has other more senior positions within it – both line (education officers) and staff (inspectors/advisers).

Proposals to deal with this situation have ranged from introducing a line manager for heads into the educational system (Trethowan 1987), to allowing heads to appraise each other by peer group review, with many suggestions between these two extremes (Hawe 1987).

The requirements of providing public credibility, being part of the management process and enjoying the confidence of heads cannot all be met. A compromise which has attracted much support is for a triumverate of an education officer, an adviser and a fellow head to play a part in the appraisal process (Suffolk Education Department 1987).

Summary

Essential features of an appraisal system

It should be part of the managerial process.
It should be positive and developmental whilst still maintaining credibility as a check on quality.
It should ultimately improve the learning experiences of pupils and students.
It should be combined with some element of career development and progression.
It should formulate training needs and professional development opportunities.
It should provide a two-way dialogue by which the appraisee gives feedback on the manager's performance and is able to raise organisational problems.
It should have an infrastructure to provide the back-up to plan and deliver training and co-ordinate professional development through experience in other parts of the organisation.

SECTION 2
APPROACHES TO APPRAISAL IN EDUCATION

2.1 Target Setting Approach: Feedback with Responsibility

David Trethowan

Performance Appraisal and Target Setting (PATS)

Feedback may be defined as the described perception of a teacher's behaviour, conduct or professional performance from any person who is affected directly or indirectly by that performance. Feedback is like advice: it can be accepted and acted upon or it can be ignored. Appraisal is the perception of that teacher's performance which is the view (collected from appropriate sources) of the appraiser responsible for the performance of that teacher. Appraisal is a special form of feedback. It is feedback from someone charged with responsibility for the teacher and his or her performance. It cannot legitimately be ignored: the appraiser has the responsibility to see that it is acted upon. Good appraisers will collate all the available feedback in order to compile as fair a view as possible of the performance. Good appraisers also will give great weight to the teacher's view of that performance, and will consider, too, any feedback the appraisee has received. Great trust is developed in the continuous formulation of termly or annual appraisals if each participant is seeking the same end of an unbiased, fair assessment of the performance given to the organisation by the appraisee over a set period. These appraisals are based upon collated feedback.

It has often seemed to me to be not unlike the fable of the 'Six Blind Men of Hindustan' describing an elephant. Feedback from any of them reveals there to be a huge body, a trunk, a tail, and if they are not all to have a misunderstanding of the total shape of an elephant, they must trust each other's feedback, pool their experiences and so come as close as possible to perfect knowledge.

There is no-one, whether inspector, governor, adviser, headteacher, or anyone at all who can provide a speedier appraisal if it is to be accurate. They are all as partially sighted as the rest of us, though their feedback can be useful in forming the appraisal.

If there is no 'all-seeing one' in appraisal, who can instantly provide for us the informed, objective and perfectly described performance, how does the appraiser know how well the teacher is performing?

The most common sources of feedback on teachers are:

1. The teacher's own view of the performance, including performance against agreed targets.

2. The appraiser's view of the performance gained from visits to lessons; checks of pupil work and assessments; departmental and one-to-one discussions, etc.

3. Feedback from those affected directly or indirectly by the teacher's performance such as pupils, parents, ancillary staff.

4. Observations of school visitors such as inspectors, advisers, or possibly LEA officers.

Most feedback collection is necessarily random. The good appraiser collects feedback openly and professionally, pooling each comment with the teacher as it becomes available, never storing it up for a surprise item at the appraisal interview. A good appraiser is professionally alert: it is neither necessary nor desirable to watch all teachers all of the time to be able to draw professionally valid conclusions about their work. That is not to say there is no occasion when a teacher would be under close scrutiny. Detailed observation is best saved for analysing an identified problem, giving guidance to improve a performance, or for the occasion when appraiser and appraisee cannot reach agreement and more research is needed to establish common ground.

In short, an accurate view of performance can only be built up by collated, continuous feedback over time. In athletics, when we want to improve the hurdler's performance, we learn more from action photographs of how he or she moves over the track, than from a snapshot of the finish. *In appraisal, we are not talking about winners and losers but about improving the performance of everyone on the track.*

One approach to the improved performance of teachers, of departments, and of whole schools, is Performance Appraisal and Target Setting (PATS). The key elements in PATS are:

1.   A clear description of the basic task required to be performed by each teacher, including an indication of the key areas on which performance will be appraised.

2.   A clearly indicated organisational structure of accountability within the school with a line manager for each teacher for that teacher's performance.

3.   The opportunity for each teacher in the school to agree targets to be achieved by him or her and to propose targets for the organisation within which he or she works.

The basic task

The year 1987 saw the appearance of the first national attempt to describe a teacher's basic task in school. In outline it is 1,265 hours of directed work plus time to discharge professional duties effectively. The key areas in which an acceptable performance is required seem from that document to be: planning, teaching, assessing, guidance, disciplining, reporting, liaison, administration and participating in school and department development. More detail will need to be added to this basic task possibly by the LEA and certainly by the school. Teachers are entitled to know what is expected of them in a standard, basic performance – the 'bottom line' which will allow the school to operate as a perfectly sound organisation and reassure the teacher that nothing more can be demanded. This basic task must be set at a high but achievable level. Teacher performances below this level will not allow the school to fulfil its legally required mission of providing full time education for all pupils of the school appropriate to their age, aptitude and ability. Such defective teacher performances become a school priority and are a matter for the teacher and his or her appraiser to resolve. First, the appraiser has to agree with the teacher that a shortfall in performance exists, if necessary, by producing appropriate feedback. In a trusting relationship it could well be the appraiser and not the teacher who has to be convinced that the teacher's performance is deficient in some respect. This is perfectly natural since there must of necessity be facets of a teacher's performance where an appraiser has little feedback to compare with that of the teacher. Few organisations pay one employee solely to watch the performance of another.

Second, a teaching performance deficient in the basic task requires action to rectify the weakness – be it advice on lesson preparation, coaching in lesson delivery, or support in making pupil skill assessment. In the interests of pupils and colleagues, as well as the teacher concerned, the basic task has to be fulfilled even if this requires an emergency solution. *The education of the child is paramount*.

Third, comes the long term, more permanent solution – the real test of a PATS system and the evidence that an organisation feels it shares the responsibility for improved teacher performance. I refer of course to training and development. I do not shirk the possibility that the deficient performer may be unwilling or unable to improve and that this may lead eventually to implementation of the LEA disciplinary procedure and to dismissal. But in almost all cases of a qualified teacher being unable to achieve the basic task, the solution is likely to lie in consultancy support; in on-the-job coaching: or in INSET courses. This may not be true of the 'target' tasks which a teacher wants to accept in addition to performing the basic task. Maybe these need to be adjusted, redefined, or even abandoned if they were inappropriately selected. *But the basic task cannot be adjusted: in that task an acceptable performance must be achieved by all*.

Line manager

Ask of each participant on a management training course of any industrial or commercial company who his or her line manager is and the name will unequivocally be given. Ask the same question on any training course for teachers and not only will the participants offer the names of at least three people but will probably launch into a debate about the whole concept of line management. In short, the concept of one teacher being accountable to another for his or her total performance in school is not widely accepted, practised or even understood. *The corollary that this line manager is responsible for the standards of performance of his or her teachers, celebrates their achievements, is their appraiser, sets targets with them and is the person to whom they are expected to turn first in times of trouble, stress or pressure, is almost never used in the education service.* John Evans in the Education for Industrial Society booklet on Delegation (Trethowan 1983) feels accountable to so many colleagues for his daily tasks that he appeals to the school hierarchy to untangle a system which puts him under so many independent pressures simultaneously. The answer under PATS is to nominate for every teacher a person to be his or her line manager. Part of the brief for this line manager is to ensure a sound performance from his or her half dozen teachers. Part of the line manager's own appraisal will be based on effectiveness in the task of managing, developing and motivating those who are accountable to him or her. Speaking generally, I have found in most instances that teachers are best managed by heads of subject departments who are in turn best managed by deputy heads who are in turn best managed by the headteacher. This is not an inflexible rule of management organisational structure, and some staff may be better managed elsewhere within the organisation. The important features which this system makes possible are:

1. The probability of close daily contacts.   Appraisal is not a once a term or year task, it is a daily availability for performance management, which is summarised once a year.

2. An understanding of the task the teacher is performing.   One of the major factors in my deciding to delegate appraisal to heads of department was their greater detailed appreciation of the task the teacher was performing. The possibility of evolving criteria acceptable to school, department and individuals on which performance can be judged is far greater under this system of departmental delegation.

3. An empathy with the teacher.   A major fear amongst teachers is appraisal by someone who does not appreciate the particular conditions under which some teachers with some classes in some schools operate. Judgment by a school 'visitor' such as an administrator, inspector or adviser unfamiliar with the ethos can be a most demotivating experience.

What are the problems with this system of school line management? Could heads of department, deputy heads and headteachers perform this role? I have no doubt that they could, given training in appraisal skills and time to collect feedback, to appraise and to coach. Many people at present in these posts in schools feel ill equipped to become appraisers. Appraisal was not a feature of the role when they accepted promotion and it will take time to train and equip them to become skilled at the appraisal task. In some promoted teachers, perfectly sound performers themselves, there is understandably neither the willingness nor the ability to be effective appraisers. Early retirements or restructuring in schools will gradually reduce the small number of unwilling appraisers. In extreme cases their role as appraisers must temporarily be borne by others in the organisation who are better equipped to do so. For the majority of promoted teachers however, a new, skilled, challenging and very rewarding task lies ahead – the nurturing, coaching and developing of a team of subordinate colleagues. Appraising and managing the personal and professional development of colleagues is at least as rewarding as any other role in the teaching profession.

Target setting

If the line management organisation and the identification of a basic task are means of ensuring a sound school, it is target setting which has the power to make a school and its staff outstanding. I have written elsewhere that target setting is not merely a management technique. It is a school management philosophy (Trethowan 1987). This philosophy assumes that people work better if they have some control over what they have to do, and work best of all if they help to suggest, define and set some of their own tasks. It also assumes that people like best to work in an effective team and organisation and that they enjoy agreed delegated, professional tasks which probably require them to have minimum supervision because the criteria for successful achievement have been agreed at the start. Such targets could be concerned with personal or professional development of the individual such as acquiring leadership training, timetabling skills, expertise in remedial work, new subject knowledge, etc. Targets could also be concerned with improving department or school performance such as creating GCSE teaching materials, taking an additional responsibility or training and coaching a colleague in a new skill. It could also mean teaching in a new subject or on a new syllabus which the school requires.
In outcome, development of the individual teacher and of the school tend to overlap in most target areas, but it is usually clear for whose benefit the target was originated.
The agreement of a teacher and the department to formulate a target implies:

1.   That the basic task of the teacher is being well achieved. If it were not, the school would require targets set to ensure the improvement of basic task performance and would probably not support any additional targets until the basic task was being achieved.

2.   That the school will support the achievement of a target in every way possible, be it funding, time, support for attendance at courses, opportunity for on-the-job training in school, room, space or any other resource.

3.   That the school expects and can depend upon the achievement of all priority targets. Targets are prioritised as essential, important, and desirable to achieve. As conditions change, teachers sometimes wish to revise targets, reducing or relinquishing the least essential by agreement with their appraiser. Failure to achieve or to agree the reduction of targets would reveal a marked lack of maturity and would not augur well for future responsibilities.

Target achievement however, presents the teacher with fresh challenges, greater motivation and a means of career management. It lifts the department and school from the safe and sound to the superb.

Is any target acceptable? Clearly targets must fall within the aims and the ethos of the school. A target proposal to spend time, money, space and resources producing materials for mixed ability classes of students of German for a school that would not be using them would be an obvious case for refusal. In practice, few targets are proposed which require rejection. Teachers closest to the action see better than most what is required and agree to meet the challenge. They do not have time to waste on irrelevant targets.

How frequent are appraisal interviews? With the academic year as the basic time unit, summative appraisal and new target setting take place with appraisals in the latter half of the summer term. A leapfrog interview (with the appraiser's appraiser) takes place in the autumn term of the new academic year. A formative appraisal with the appraiser again takes place in the spring term. Interviews are personal and private and try to follow the accumulated wisdom on appraisal interviews concerning timing, preparation, advance notice, briefing, interview planning, listening skills, etc. Appropriate documentation should help and not hinder all stages of the process, preparation interview and follow-up (Trethowan 1987).

PATS represents a sizable investment of a school's resources. How is that investment incorporated into school policy:

1.   PATS is integrated into the school planning and review system whereby at least once a year each department and its staff undertake a comprehensive review.

2.   PATS is the link between staff development and organisation development. Through constructive discussion, efforts are made to reconcile and balance differences and to identify common targets.

3.   PATS is a means of identifying and solving some of the school's problems and the means of managing change. All funds above basic capitation are allocated through this system.

4.   PATS is the focus of school staff development, as a result of which teacher development needs are identified and on-the-job or off-site training and development activities are agreed.

5.   PATS is a major means of communication especially upward and downward communication along lines of management, but also in all directions on any school issue.

The most commonly used interview style is a participative one. Fortunately most people feel comfortable with this style and need guidelines only to reinforce the appropriate attitude. These are:
–Listen to what is being said, to what is being left unsaid and to what needs your help to be said.
–Ask questions to clarify and summarise, to encourage, talk, or to guide the discussion towards a topic which is being avoided.
–Do not argue, give gratuitous advice or 'pull rank'.
–Respect confidentiality and agree how much of a discussion can be included in a written record.

There are occasions for using other management styles including telling, selling and delegation, but mainly these will be outside the appraisal interview room and are the exceptions inside it.
The benefits of PATS are immense. For the teacher it clarifies the role and task, not only for the newcomer, but as a reminder to the long established. The system requires the teacher be given feedback on performance, to be thanked for good work and to have stress relieved through discussion of problems. The target setting component allows the teacher to control additional input, confident that any agreed additional efforts will be valued and supported by the school. The record of basic task performance and targets will form the predictable basis of a confidential reference in promotion discussions.

The benefits to the organisation are equally clear. PATS identifies and solves problems providing a process for the management of change. It encourages teachers to learn the work tasks of appropriate colleagues to support their career development so providing a plan for short-term cover and long-term succession for all posts above the main professional grade. It encourages teamwork within departments. Longest lasting of all is its positive effects upon staff relationships and the feeling of a caring school.

The LEA gains from PATS also. The close detailed discussion leads to improved planning and better use of resources. The potential of staff is maximised and training needs are identified and met through school development programmes and an effective Grant Related In-Service Training (GRIST) funded programme. PATS would also produce reliable feedback on the success of training and development. It should also reassure LEAs that effective control is being exercised in schools.

The greatest potential weakness in the system is the lack of an appraiser similarly close to the headteacher as a head of department can be to a teacher. Appraisal is not a once-a-year task, it is an ongoing professional management relationship. The appraiser guides, advises, corrects and encourages all year and agrees a summary of the year's performance at the appraisal interview. Who performs this for the headteacher? Not HM Inspectorate, for they have no powers, no line management relationship with heads and do not appraise any individual. Not the LEA, whose advisers only advise and whose chief officers have never in my case set me or my school any form of educational target or given any form of feedback. Not the governing body, even under the Education Act of 1986. Governors continue to lack the time, the expertise and the power to manage the performance of headteachers. *Britain is the only advanced, civilised nation not to have the equivalent of a school superintendent managing the performance of its state sector headteachers.* Consequently schools gather their aims where they will.

None of this, however, detracts from the effectiveness of PATS within a school. Once a school knows what is its mission, and many of them do, it can operate an effective PATS system. But if the nation's schools should have their aims identified nationally, the circle of accountability would be complete: the elected government, the ministry, school superintendents, headteachers and their staffs would give back to the electorate the education it demanded. There would be no missing link. The whole education system would be subject to 'feedback with responsibility'.

2.2 The Staff Development Approach to Appraisal

David Styan

Introduction

Appraisal is no new concept in education. There are times when it would appear that there are those who believe it is an alien idea, developed in industry and commerce, and sprung upon an unsuspecting teaching profession in recent years. Yet schools are where everyone experiences their first formal appraisals, administered and devised by teachers. Teachers appraise their students all the time, both formally and informally. And they themselves are appraised, both by their students, and by their superiors. Every time an appointment is made to a new post, or school, staff are appraised, as they were through their teacher training and probationary year. Only those who, once fully certificated, have never applied for promotion can be said to have been free of formal appraisal. But informal appraisal has been the regular activity of staff, parents, pupils, advisers and administrators since schools began.

Staff development

The same is true of staff development. Much modern literature is written as if staff development only began when in-service training courses became so widespread in the 1970s. It is true that the growth of teachers' centres, management centres, and advisory services, along with a heightened awareness in higher education that initial training of teachers is not enough in a profession that is facing rapid change, has led to many more teachers receiving formal developmental experience. But it is also obvious that the main way in which staff develop their capacities is not by off-site activities, but from doing the job. Long before even the lively growth of largely self-generated school-based staff development programmes in the late 1970s, teachers learnt their trade, received guidance and encouragement, stricture and even condemnation from senior colleagues. Schools, especially before the introduction of a steeply hierarchical payments system under the Burnham agreements, expected staff to demonstrate that they could cope with teaching and administration by the way they did their job, and then promoted them to deputy and head if they were thought to have the potential to do these jobs. Most, if not all, who have reached headship could cite an influential figure who had provided the confidence-boosting word at a crucial moment, taken them under the wing, and, if not by design, then by accident, provided the opportunity to show what the individual could do.

So schools have always been learning environments, for both children and the staff, and written references, a more significant element in staff selection than is the case in many careers, have always represented formal appraisal of the strengths and weaknesses of teachers. If there is such a long acquaintance with appraisal, why, then, is there such a wide degree of disquiet in the staffrooms of this country at present? It can hardly be that teachers are content to be judged on an ad hoc, capricious, secretive way, unable to have access to written references, dependent upon chance encounter and discussions with their senior colleagues to determine their worth for promotion, salary enhancement or even in-service opportunity. Yet even in those schools, many more now than even five years ago, that have devised a coherent programme of staff development, open references, regular discussions, written records, and their own in-service schemes, there is a suspicion about a national framework of appraisal.

Apprehension about appraisal

It may be, of course, that the apprehension is simply a reaction to the unknown. Teachers, uncertain about the precise form that appraisal may take, and doubting the credentials of those who may appraise them, let alone the consequences of such appraisal, may be anxious only about the unfamiliar. They certainly can receive reassurance from the fact that all the associations that represent teachers are on record as being in favour of a national framework for appraisal.

Indeed, in a period when there has been more division and acrimony amongst these groups than ever before, appraisal stands out as an area of ready agreement between them, and also, with their employers, the LEAs, and the DES.

With a cultural background which is increasingly recognising a staff development policy as an essential characteristic of a thinking school, it seems more likely that the worries associated with the national framework of appraisal and its implementation are more to do with ideas of control, accountability, reward, promotion, and dismissal than with professional development. For, whilst there is an acceptance that you cannot have staff development without an element of appraisal, there are forms of appraisal that can be introduced that do not foster staff development. Staff development uses appraisal processes to improve the level of performance of teachers for the benefit of children in their care. But there are other motives for appraisal. Its imposition by the Education No. 2 Act (1986), and the Teachers' Pay and Conditions of Service Act (1987), rather than its encouragement as a voluntary activity in itself suggests other purposes than performance improvement. It is clear from the new means of allocating allowances for teachers above the main grade that the concept of merit pay is now part of the system in England and Wales, and this reward for outstanding classroom teachers implies that an appraisal system serves the purpose of identifying such teachers. It is difficult to envisage that the national appraisal framework will not be linked to the general allocation of allowances, or that it will have no bearing upon moves to accelerate the removal of those teachers who are not thought to be suitable.

In summary, appraisal can be used, and is used, in other careers, and other countries, like parts of the United States of America, for teachers, to determine pay, promotions and dismissal. Appraisal is also a necessary part of staff development, but it is not yet clear whether a system can be operated that achieves the latter without creating deep suspicions that it is really about the other purposes. And if staff see it as a judgemental process, determining pay and promotion, and threatening job security, their approach to being made to take part will be a highly defensive and suspicious one. It will not be surprising if teachers quickly adopt the negative attitudes to appraisal all too commonly found in existing schemes elsewhere: denigration of the personnel, and the results; window-dressing to impress; a readiness to challenge perceived distortions; and a cynical reaction to critical appraisal.

The control model

This depressing prospect is not, however, inevitable. It does seem likely to occur if the framework adopted borrows inappropriate models from industry, and if the tone is thoroughly hierarchical. To show what could be the experience for the teaching profession, it is necessary to describe a possible model, the *control* model, based upon a view of the schools that owes much to hierarchical thinking. This model sees senior management within schools as having a role in making teachers more effective, and needs appraisal as a tool to require teachers to aim for targets and achieve objectives because of the need to answer questions from one's superiors.

Such a model would have a number of clear characteristics; it would be a 'top-down' model with appraisal being conducted by heads, or heads of departments for their subordinates, the assistant teachers. This 'in-line' process sees the more senior person sitting in judgement over the more junior. The element of accountability would be high, with detailed job specifications against which performance can be measured. The tendency to try to measure so often leads to valuing that which can be so measured, but it must be asked whether there are measures that exist that accurately capture the quality of teaching and learning. Even the apparently simple work of codifying the whole of teachers' tasks is more difficult than first appears. A hierarchical approach also involves the accountability going beyond the school to others, e.g. the LEA, governors, etc. A hierarchical approach tends to look for results to justify judgements, and since appraisers are not colleagues but superiors, often results in appraisal of a snapshot kind. Failure to achieve targets set will, over time, lead inevitably to dismissal. This whole approach draws heavily upon the notion that those in authority are able to train or develop others, and can accurately appraise the work of their staffs.

Before considering an alternative model, it is worth asking how appropriate a hierarchical model is to the activity of a school. It can be argued that not only do we have an hierarchical system operating in our schools, but that this is an appropriate system to have. Certainly, the imposed settlement of the longest dispute in the education system is one that emphasises hierarchical structures, and the government, with some support from heads, has urged the need for what it calls a managerial structure to run our schools. The five allowances above main grade and below deputy headship contrast with the two such grades that were the basis of the ACAS agreement between the employers and most teacher associations. It can be said that schools, especially large ones, with hundreds of children, and often well over a hundred adults, must be run by a hierarchy; that they are essentially bureaucracies, and should be seen in terms of maintaining a sound organisation in the interests of the children. It is claimed that, notwithstanding the views of the association leaders, most teachers in staffrooms resent the erosion of differentials now, as they did when the Houghton settlement removed a grade from the range of allowances, and that schools need chains of command, with clear responsibilities arranged along an 'in-line' pattern, or otherwise, they would be difficult to control. If we know what we are doing, and have evolved a satisfactory system of instruments that achieve these ends, we would be justified, as a profession, in arguing for such a structure. And yet, there is ample evidence that this is not so. In the crucial issues of 'what is education for?' and 'how can it best be achieved?', let alone 'how big should schools be?', 'how should they be organised?' and 'how can we best effect change?', the answers are not available, or if they are they are, far from being universally accepted. At a time when change is the prevailing climate, and there are new ideas and initiatives each week to seek better answers, schools are run by bureaucratic systems best applied to manufacturing technologically static products, or servicing an unchanging need.

It is obvious, particularly in the work of those like Professor Charles Handy who have analysed schools as institutions from an industrial background (Handy 1984), that schools are still structured on a factory, or army-type model, at precisely the time that they need a far more flexible, inventive, and professional mode. Hierarchical systems flourish best when we know what we want to do, and know how best to do it; so it suits manufacturing where to change production methods dramatically is technologically difficult or financially prohibitive. It is also an efficient system when change is demanded, but the institutions themselves are unwilling or unable to change. They are effective structures for enforced change, and there is little doubt that frequent references to enhancing the power and control of the head, and the separation of heads and deputies from the rest of the staff in the new contracts of employment, are both devices for enforcing change. The 'right to manage' is a slogan that reflects the desire of those in authority to override those in subordinate positions in a time of change.

What hierarchies are totally inappropriate for, is the process of internally generated change; if real change is to occur in the interests of the quality of children's learning, then it must be internalised, and thoroughly accepted, not evaded, by teachers. It is said by the Secretary of State that education must be rescued from being producer-dominated and become consumer-dominated. Leaving aside the question of who is the consumer, parent, child or society, there is little evidence available that consumer-domination will necessarily improve quality.

Telling schools what to do, and how to do it may be a favourite pastime, but achieves little without engaging the professional commitment of teachers. The fact is that the learning processes, insofar as they are thoroughly understood by anyone, are more subtle, more individual, more complex than a consumer-dominated view would suggest. *Imperatives that demand 'standards', and that children should achieve certain levels, achieve nothing.* You do not get 'better teachers', or 'better schools' by demanding better teachers and better schools. *Issuing instructions, paying new allowances, and imposing appraisal schemes does not, in itself, achieve anything, if the teachers are not fully committed to what is being done, and involved in devising its delivery.*

If we start by asking what is the most appropriate climate for learning, a process that is fundamentally one of enquiry, curiosity, critical awareness and high motivation to learn, it is obvious that a mechanistic, in-line management model, is out of sympathy with this activity. Such a model serves well the needs of an instructional process; it is appropriate for training skills, but drilling and learning are not the same activity. If we want to educate by rote, we will produce robots, but if we want mature people, we have to value the questioning, the unorthodox, problem-solving approaches.

In these circumstances, those organisations that succeed are ones where a group of professionals, sharing a common goal embark on close relationships with the clients, confident that they, not the system, deliver the 'product', i.e. the education of each child. If education is essentially an individual process undertaken in a social context, then its organisation should stress this, and each teacher be seen as the key element. Another way of saying the same thing is this: industrial experience has much to say to schools, but transplanting the managerial structure of a firm making cars to a school is not an example of such experience, and nor is an appraisal scheme based upon in-line management, and hierarchical assessment and accountability.

There are, then, models for running organisations based upon hierarchical structures that are effective for preserving the status quo, or for enforced change, and as a tool of such a system, a mechanistic, appraisal scheme is very useful. Its character is set out in Figure 1, and it flourishes in a climate of clear aims, external power, subordination, and obedience. If applied to schools, such an approach will foster time-serving, compliance, window-dressing, and attention to the measurable. If that is the type of education system needed for the end of the 20th century, and for the first half of the 21st century, then such an appraisal system based on target-setting, external validation, assessment and judgments is also required.

Professional development model

However, there is an alternative. This is to expand and encourage the
existing culture, and use a professional development model (see
Figure 3). This approach, enthusiastically adopted by the teacher
associations, supported by the work with the Suffolk authority, and
developed in the submissions of several LEAs in their applications to
be national pilot schemes, is the one that can achieve teacher involvement. A development model can command respect because good
teachers recognize it as the one they practise with their students, and
the one that encourages learning. It is the model that represents
extension of good practice, not imposition of inappropriate practice
from elsewhere. Such a developmental, rather than a judgemental
approach, has clear characteristics, which can be simply summarised.
These are that the initiative comes from within the operational institution, the school. This 'bottom-up' approach involves professionals
coming together on the basis of a shared commitment to improving
the education of the children in their care. This collegiate atmosphere
means that the staff as a whole devises the appropriate mechanisms
for a systematic appraisal scheme in each school, based upon self-
evaluation, self-motivation for improvement, and a readiness to help
each other. If there exists mutual respect, and organisational trust,
then staff will meet each other to negotiate targets, and appraise each
other. All such appraisal would be two-way, incorporating self-
appraisal, peer appraisal, superior and subordinate appraisal, so arriving at a more rounded perception by the individual concerned. All
would share in the enhanced performance of each other, feel thoroughly involved in designing as well as carrying out the scheme, and
see appraisal, firmly based in the school, as a continuous activity. The
main role of the most senior members of staff is in facilitating in-service
training, extended experience, and observation to enhance understanding of what can be achieved. The LEA has an obvious role in
servicing this aspect of the work. This model is one of personal growth.
It requires tact, and skill, time, and resources, and certainly is neither
bland nor parochial if properly conducted. Its participants need training in discussion and observational skills, as well as confidence-
building techniques. Given such an approach, teachers can gain in
professional status and performance, without feeling threatened, and
children will gain as a result.

Conclusion

Staff development is already a vital part of the school scene. It faces
the serious threat of being elbowed out by a hard-nosed appraisal

THE CONTROL MODEL

C O N T R O L

STAFF APPRAISAL (OR ASSESSMENT)
EXTERNAL ACCOUNTABILITY
TRAINER/DEVELOPMENT ROLES
SUBORDINATES RECEIVE APPRAISAL
VALUES THE MEASURABLE
SUPERIORS APPRAISE
EXTERNALLY IMPOSED
FAILURE MEANS DISMISSAL
'SNAP-SHOT' OPINIONS
RELATED TO REWARDS
APPRAISAL BY RESULTS
TARGET SETTING
HIERARCHIAL
TOP DOWN

J U D G E M E N T A L

MOTIVATION FROM PROFESSIONAL STATUS
RELATED TO CURRENT PEPFORMANCE
PROFESSIONAL DEVELOPMENT
INTERNAL ACCOUNTABILITY
WEAKNESSES WORKED ON
COLLEGIATE APPROACH
SUPERIORS APPRAISE
VALUE THE PERCEPTIVE
TARGETS NEGOTIATED
CONTINUOUS APPRAISAL
SELF MOTIVATION
TWO WAY APPRAISAL
INSTITUTION BASED
LOCAL SCHEMES
BOTTOM UP

G R O W T H

D E V E L O P M E N T A L

THE GROWTH MODEL

Figure 3 – The control and growth models

package that owes more to putting teachers in their place, than to
ensuring they are better teachers when they get there. ***Development
is a positive and vital educative process and lies at the essence of
what schools are for. Control is a negative, and belittling process***

when applied to a group of professionals who themselves have the responsibility for guiding young people entrusted to them. If the young people of this country are to be educated by time-serving subordinates, eager to create a good impression , or demoralised by ill-founded appraisal of their performance, rewarded by being marked out from their colleagues, and valued for their conformity to measurable norms, the children will be sold short. Unlike industrial production, they cannot be recycled or scrapped. We need to get it right from the start.

2.3 The Role of the LEA

Joan Dean

Introduction

The new conditions of service for teachers include a requirement for teachers for 'participating in any arrangements within an agreed national framework for the appraisal of his performance and that of other teachers'. The conditions of service for heads contain a similar clause. Schools will therefore need to set up appraisal schemes if they have not done so already and LEAs will need to advise, monitor, support and evaluate these schemes, provide appraisal for head teachers and deal with the problems which will inevitably arise.

Appraisal is not a process which should be seen in isolation. It should be seen as part of the much wider process of staff development. The LEA and the school need a policy for staff development which encompasses appraisal and sets it clearly into this context. Only if teachers see it in this way is it likely to have any effect on what happens in individual classrooms.

Desmond Nuttall, speaking at a conference in Sheffield in March 1986 (BERA 1986) suggested that the characteristics of a successful appraisal scheme were similar to the characteristics of a successful self-appraisal scheme. It required above all an atmosphere of trust among the staff concerned, a good professional self image and commitment to appraisal from the top and willingness to undergo it.

This suggests that the LEA staff development policy needs to encompass all its employees and not just teachers. Officers and advisers need to be appraised as part of their development and this should be known to teachers. The aim should be to make all the employees of the LEA feel part of a large overall programme for developing the work of schools by developing the work of those who are responsible for them. There are also a number of establishments in most authorities which need to be involved as well as schools and colleges, e.g. teachers' centres, special needs units, adult education centres, etc.

It is also the case that the better the relationships within the LEA between officers, advisers and teachers, the more effectively can the LEA promote and participate in the process of appraisal. The worst situation will be one where teachers feel that the scheme is being imposed upon them from above.

The responsibility of the LEA

If the requirement in the new conditions of service is to be carried out, it is the responsibility of the LEA to see that appraisal happens in all its schools and other establishments. We do not yet know what will be laid down in the national scheme and from this point of view it is difficult to assess what will be the LEA responsibility. The list of tasks given below is thus a list of tasks which **might** be undertaken by the LEA.

1. Setting out an authority staff development policy which includes appraisal as an integral part of the development process.

2. Defining what is meant by appraisal and what will be involved in the appraisal process within the authority.

3. Providing guidelines which will help schools and other establishments in setting up appraisal, which lay down the parameters within which it will take place.

4. Sharing this thinking with staff in schools and other establishments and ensuring that all staff understand what is involved.

5. Providing in-service training for officers, advisers, heads and senior staff in schools and other establishments, likely to be involved in the appraisal process.

6. Encouraging headteachers and staff to work together in the design of their strategy of appraisal; encouraging schools to draw up criteria for classroom observation, review of other contributions and teacher assessment, having regard to the nature of individual posts and particular teacher skills. Providing suggestions for this from which schools and other establishments can select.

7. Providing a system of appraisal for headteachers which takes into account the varied nature of a headteacher's responsibilities.

8.   Moderating the scheme, through the advisory service, ensuring that staff and headteachers share in the setting up and monitoring of appraisal and seeing that appropriate reports are produced; ensuring that there is some consistency of standards between schools while allowing for local differences.

9.   Dealing with any appeals stemming from appraisals.

10. Ensuring that there is appropriate follow-up to the appraisal.

11. Evaluating the scheme and making any improvements necessary.

12. Providing the resources needed for appraisal.

Each of these tasks can be considered in detail:

(i)   *Setting out an authority staff development policy which includes appraisal as an integral part of the development process*

We have already noted that an LEA staff development policy needs to concern all employees of the LEA There is a need for commitment to the idea that everyone should develop in his or her work and a corresponding intention to make resources available for this development as far as possible.

The policy also needs to contain an intention to assess needs and make provision in the light of them. This involves reviewing the age and qualifications of teachers against the needs of the authority, looking to see how far these two match and how any discrepancy between them can be made good.

It also involves taking into account what teachers see as their needs and providing opportunities in the light of them. This may be done by allocating money to individual schools or groups of schools or through the funds made available to teachers' centres for programmes requested by teachers. Information will also come from groups of teacher representatives whether these are union representatives or an in-service committee.

Part of the policy will involve consideration of how the programme is divided between short courses and workshops and long course provision.

Staff development is not only a matter of providing in-service training. For most teachers the best learning comes as part of the everyday classroom work and an LEA can encourage schools to look at ways of developing teachers by allowing them to visit other schools or watch other teachers at work, by exchanging jobs with other teachers or acting as deputy to someone in a particular job for a period in order to learn the job. Exchanges of teachers between schools in the LEA may offer development opportunities and so may secondment for tasks needed by the LEA but requiring study. For example in one LEA, teachers were seconded for periods ranging from a term to a year to study the provision for gifted students at sixth form level, to review the current state of science in the secondary schools in the authority, to provide archive material for GCSE, and many other things.

Appraisal, then, becomes one of the ways in which the school and the LEA decides on its needs. One of the problems about this is that it is not easy for the LEA to collect the information coming from the appraisal of individual teachers in each school and although some of their needs can be met through provision at teachers' centres where they have some say in what is provided, a good deal may need to be met through the resources of the schools. It therefore seems important to make provision for schools to develop some of their own in-service training.

(ii)   *Defining what is meant by appraisal and what will be involved in the appraisal process within the authority*

Appraisal can mean a variety of different things. The LEA needs to have an overall view of what it considers appraisal to be if it is to be able to support and help schools in implementing appraisal pro- grammes. Some of this may be laid down nationally, but there will undoubtedly be areas in which the LEA needs to issue guidelines.

A useful definition is given by the Secondary Heads' Association (1984) which regards appraisal as:

A systematic review of performance and potential as part of a full scheme of personal and professional staff development.

The LEA also needs to make decisions about the following:

(a)   The basis on which teachers will be appraised, i.e. Is there to be classroom observation? What evidence of a teachers's performance should be taken into account?

(b)   The frequency of the appraisal interview for teachers at different stages of their careers.

(c)   Who appraises whom? A decision is needed about whether peer group appraisal is acceptable or whether appraisal should be by someone senior to the teacher being appraised.

(d)   What might be suggested for inclusion in the appraisal interview. One authority, for example, suggested that the interview should cover the following:
   –   Feedback on observation.
   –   Assessment of performance including:
       recognition of achievement; identification of areas for development; setting of targets for future performance; identification of ways in which the school can contribute to the teacher's development.
   –   Assessment of potential.
   –   An opportunity to discuss problems.
   –   An opportunity to provide feedback to the appraiser.
   –   An action plan.

(e)   Schools will also need advice on reporting and the LEA needs to make a statement about what is required, whether there is to be a written report, who should hold it, who should have access to it and how long it should be kept. It will also be helpful to schools to have some guidance on whether appraisal reports furnish information for confidential reports on teachers who are candidates for promotion. It is difficult to see how this can be avoided since the head in writing a confidential report cannot forget what he or she knows from the appraisal but it needs discussion and agreement with teachers.

(f)   It is also important at an early stage to come to some conclusion about whether appraisal has any part in disciplinary processes. It is generally considered that it would be detrimental to the success of an appraisal scheme for teachers to fear that what they say might be used in evidence against them in a disciplinary enquiry, but it needs to be made clear that this should not happen. The LEA also needs to consider whether a teacher may use appraisal evidence in a disciplinary enquiry.

(iii)   *Providing guidelines which will help schools and other establishments in setting up appraisal, which lay down the parameters within which it will take place*

Appraisal guidelines need to set out for schools and other establishments the parameters within which the LEA wishes appraisal to take place. They also need to offer advice on how to do it, in terms which allow each school to find a pattern which suits it.

Information in the guidelines might include suggestions for classroom observation, comment on some of the other aspects of a teacher's work which might be considered in appraisal (particularly for those teachers with management responsibility), an account of the skills involved in appraisal interviewing, and information about the LEA view on reporting. Some mention should also be made of any appeals procedure.

The material in the guidelines should complement material and information given in the course of training.

(iv)   *Sharing this thinking with staff in schools and other establishments and ensuring that all staff understand what is involved*

Different authorities will wish to do this in different ways. In some LEAs, members and the CEO may wish to lay down the parameters within which the schools will work. In others this may be left very much to the advisory service and the schools to work out together the best way forward.

Whatever the arrangement, teachers need to share with the officers and advisers of the authority the plans being put forward. This may be a matter of setting up working parties to devise guidelines and a scheme for the authority or guidelines and a scheme may be put forward for discussion and modification. Either way it is essential that LEA staff and teachers work together.

Some of the discussion will be with teachers' organisations but it is important that there is also discussion with a wider group – perhaps through meetings of all headteachers who may then be given the task of talking with their staffs.

Throughout this process it must be remembered that appraisal tends to be seen by teachers who have not experienced it as a rather threatening process. The more they are told about it and the more they become familiar with the idea, the less threatening does it become.

(v)   *Providing in-service training for officers, advisers, heads and senior staff in schools and other establishments, likely to be involved in the appraisal process*

The training which will be required for appraisal is very substantial. If an authority takes seriously the overall pattern of staff development involved, all senior officers and advisory staff will require training in the skills of appraisal as well as all teachers in senior posts. The process of training will need to be continuous, catering each year for those who are new to management posts.

Training should involve practical experience in the skills involved both in classroom and other observation and in appraisal interviewing. Three days seems to be the minimum time in which appropriate training can be achieved.

It should also be noted that there is at present a shortage of people who have the skills to train others in appraisal and it seems likely that authorities will need to use a cascade model which implies training trainers as well as training people in the skills needed.

Heads of secondary schools may also need to train their middle and senior management in the skills of appraisal in the early stages since the size of the training task is likely to mean that only heads can be trained in the first instance.

However we look at it, the training involved in bringing in appraisal will be very costly in the first instance.

(vi) *Encouraging headteachers and staff to work together in the design of their strategy of appraisal; encouraging schools to draw up criteria for classroom observation, review of other contributions and teacher assessment, having regard to the nature of individual posts and particular teacher skills. Providing suggestions for this from which schools and other establishments can select*

If teachers are to be happy with appraisal they will need to be involved in the design of the appraisal pattern in their own schools. Discussion about what is involved in classroom observation and agreement about what is to be observed make the process much more acceptable and valuable. The way in which other contributions to the school are reviewed also needs discussion and teachers with management responsibilities need to agree how they will be assessed. The appraisal interview itself will be less threatening when its form and content are discussed and agreed so that both parties know where they stand.

If it is to be effective, appraisal needs to involve a large measure of self-assessment as part of the preparation for the appraisal interview. This needs to be discussed in schools and other establishments and in many cases it will be helpful to provide a framework to aid this process. The LEA can help here by encouraging heads to undertake this kind of discussion, perhaps building ideas about it into training programmes. The LEA may also provide possible patterns and outlines of forms of observation and self-assessment from which schools can select.

(vii) *Providing a system of appraisal for headteachers which takes into account the varied nature of a headteacher's responsibilities*

Providing appraisal for headteachers is the most difficult part of introducing an appraisal scheme. The head's role is complex, involving work with a number of different groups of people and it is not easy for any one person to undertake the evaluation of this.

A number of suggestions has been made. One is that heads should be appraised by their staffs. This is acceptable to a number of heads but seems unlikely to meet the requirements of a number of LEAs and of government plans. There would also seem to be disadvantages in that teachers depend on the head for references and the process could be seen as too inward-looking.

Teachers' organisations have taken the view that anyone appraising a head should have been a head him or herself and the possibility of using retired heads or heads seconded for the purpose have been put forward. The first Suffolk study, **Those Having Torches** (Suffolk Education Department 1985), suggested that a special group of people should be recruited for this purpose.

The difficulty with all these suggestions is that the people concerned will not know the school in the first instance and will have to spend time getting to know it. *They also have no responsibility for it and are not in a position to do anything about what they find.*

The second Suffolk study (Suffolk Education Department 1987) suggests that possibly a trio of officer, adviser and fellow head might do an appraisal together. This covers the ground well but is very expensive in terms of the time of those concerned. An officer or adviser with responsibility for schools within an area of an authority may well have over a hundred schools to cover. In the costing given in the second study the appraisal of heads would amount to 3,000 hours for three people, which would mean that the officer concerned would be spending more than half his time on appraisal.

The advisory service is undertaking appraisal in some authorities. There is some doubt about this, depending upon the view of its advisory service the heads in an authority hold. The comment is made that not enough advisers have been head teachers. This might be translated to mean that heads are not satisfied that some advisers would be competent to undertake this task, while others would, including some who have not been heads. It may be that advisory services will need to identify a small number among them who would be acceptable to the heads in their area. Most services would need to be augmented to be able to undertake this and they would need to spend time talking with others about the way a head works in the areas they do not encounter such as relationships with governors.

(viii)   *Moderating the scheme, through the advisory service, ensuring that staff and headteachers share in the setting up and monitoring of appraisal and seeing that appropriate reports are produced; ensuring that there is some consistency of standards between schools while allowing for local differences*

If schools are to be given a fair amount of freedom in devising their programmes of appraisal so that they can feel that it is their own scheme, there will need to be some moderation both of schemes and of the outcome of schemes. The LEA will need to be sure that the way in which each school is implementing the scheme is adequate and that the way it is working out in each school is having a beneficial effect. This will be largely a job for the advisory services who will need to look at the schemes in schools in the LEA and find ways of sampling the effect of appraisal. This again will be a substantial job for a service which is already overloaded.

(ix) *Dealing with any appeals stemming from appraisal*

There will inevitably be those who are unhappy with their appraisal. Initially this should be dealt with inside the school, and the LEA may need to set down as part of the guidelines some rules about what happens in this case, but there will also need to be the opportunity for teachers to appeal to someone outside the school. This again looks like a task for the advisory service.

(x) *Ensuring that there is appropriate follow-up to the appraisal*

There should be a number of outcomes from appraisal. In particular there will be teachers needing particular kinds of experience and particular forms of in-service provision as a result of considering their work with someone else. The LEA needs to find ways of providing for as much of this demand as possible.

As we noted earlier there are problems about this. In-service provision is planned in advance on the basis of overall perceived needs and it may be that the needs of individuals do not coincide with the programme being offered. Some needs of individuals may be met by using courses and programmes outside the authority and a good deal of development should take place by using opportunities within the school for observing other teachers, taking responsibilities of various kinds, being involved in working groups, etc. Schools may also be able to provide for the needs of their staff by the programmes they themselves set out.

LEAs will have to watch the problems which arise from this aspect of appraisal.

(xi)   *Evaluating the scheme and making any improvements necessary*

Once appraisal is established it will be necessary for the LEA to evaluate what is happening in various ways and to do anything which seems necessary to improve the scheme. Any scheme tends to become tired after a while and it may be necessary to find ways of rejuvenating it after a few years.

This seems likely to be a task for the advisory service, but would appear to be difficult with the present workload. It may be that LEAs should buy in some appraisal once the scheme is established.

(xii)   *Providing the resources needed for appraisal*

LEAs are the major providers of resources for schemes in their schools. In this situation there is hope that there will be government money for appraisal since it looks to be an extremely expensive activity.

The second Suffolk study suggests an overall cost of £125 per teacher and within the range £600-£1,100 per headteacher. This includes the cost of initial training which will become less after the first programme. The figures include observation of three 40 minute lessons, half an hour for writing up and the equivalent of an hour and three quarters interview with each teacher. Headship appraisal includes the costs of three people spending between nine and 17 hours in observation, reading and interviewing for each school, plus clerical time.

On this basis, in an authority with 50 secondary schools and 400 primary schools staffed by 6,000 teachers, the cost of teacher and headteacher appraisal will thus be over £1 million.

How far it will be possible for LEAs to find this kind of money for teacher appraisal depends a good deal on how much government contribution is offered.

Conclusion

The cost of appraisal must lead us to think very carefully about whether the effect it will have will be value for money. Appraisal at its best is undoubtedly stimulating to those involved and can have very valuable results. It is not only useful for the person being appraised but also provides an opportunity for the person doing the appraisal to see from a different point of view. It is a good training opportunity in terms of the suggestions that can be made and the way in which different developments in a school can be linked. It is one of the ways in which those who manage influence others and conversely it gives the opportunity for teachers at all levels to influence the management of the school.

On the other hand appraisal undertaken by those who are doubtful about its value and unskilled in carrying it out is likely to have a negative effect. Many teachers in secondary schools, in particular, are concerned about the possibility of being appraised by heads of departments who may lack appropriate skill.

We have in appraisal an idea which has great potential for good. It is the task of the LEA to see that as many schools as possible develop schemes which come into the positive rather than the negative category.

SECTION 3
CURRENT APPRAISAL PRACTICE IN SCHOOLS AND COLLEGES

3.0 Introduction

Brian Fidler

For a few years some individual schools have carried out activities which could loosely be called staff appraisal. The term has not been clearly defined and so a variety of practices ranging from staff development interviews to teacher assessment by classroom visiting have been included within the title. A number of schemes began in connection with staff development practices and have gradually acquired the label of appraisal.

How widespread such practices are is not easy to say. One survey which also tried to assess the number of schools about to implement appraisal schemes discovered, in a follow-up, how difficult it is to get reliable data at a time of teacher action (James and Mackenzie 1986). A further complication is that a number of schools have postponed introducing schemes until there is further guidance from either the DES or their LEA. An initial survey of 206 comprehensive schools in seven LEAs in 1984 by James and Newman (1985) which used a postal questionnaire reported that 46 schemes were in operation; 22% of schools. On the other hand the Leverhulme project at the Open University had details of only 56 schemes in England and Wales from primary and secondary schools and colleges (Turner and Clift 1985). Partly these differences reflect the nature of the data collection methods, but they may also reflect differences of interpretation of what is meant by appraisal. HMI investigating schools where initiatives in evaluation and appraisal were known to have taken place found only three of nine primary schools were practising a form of staff appraisal and only six of 12 secondary schools (DES 1985). These schools were not chosen randomly but were chosen because they were expected to display this sort of activity.

It may, therefore, be far too early to expect reliable and valid information to give any impression of the national picture. It is also debatable at this stage, when there is considerable uncertainty about the nature of appraisal and associated procedures, whether it is worthwhile to try to generalise. What may be much more useful are rather more detailed studies of individual schools. Some have already been published and we provide here details for the interested reader.

David Trethowan has described the development of the target-setting approach at Warden Park School (Trethowan 1986). Geoffrey Samuel has, over a number of years, traced the development of a system at Heathlands School from a staff development review to a formal assessment of performance (Samuel 1982, 1983, 1984a, 1984b). A system at Queen's School allowed appraisees to choose their appraiser from a panel (Bunnell and Stephens 1984). In the publication from the Better Schools Evaluation and Appraisal Conference (DES 1986) there are short descriptions of systems in two secondary schools and two primary schools. A further primary system is described by Sandbrook (1987).

The remainder of this section provides case-studies of appraisal systems in two primary schools, two secondary schools and two colleges.

CURRENT APPRAISAL PRACTICE: PRIMARY SCHOOLS

3.1   A Toe in the Water: a Tentative Step Towards Staff Appraisal

Joyce A. Hill

Introduction

It began, not as an attempt to introduce an appraisal system, but rather as a strategy for school rationalisation and organisational development. Having had five year's experience as a primary headteacher, the writer moved to a second headship, where she was confronted by a complex situation, riddled with micropolitical tensions.

The establishment, which had 360 on roll and a staff of 16, served a suburban area made up of mainly skilled manual and professional workers. It was the largest school in the district, and enjoyed a good deal of parental support. Its reputation was high locally and this was based largely upon the traditional standards and successes of selection examination days.

Approximately five years previously, an amalgamation had taken place of the former junior and infant schools, under the junior headteacher. The majority of staff were well-established, many having been there for more than 10 years, and a number had never taught anywhere else. Many undercurrents were detectable, and the situation was not eased by a basic suspicion that existed regarding the differing educational philosophies supported by the two departments. Fundamentally, standards within traditional subject areas were sound, but the curriculum was narrow, with the emphasis being placed on content and presentation rather than the learning process.

Early developments

It was obvious from the writer's earliest days there, that many staff were ready to make a far greater professional contribution to the school, and were prepared to evaluate what was happening, and be self-critical if necessary. There were others, however, who were largely satisfied with the status quo, and saw little reason for changing what, to them, were highly successful practices.

If there were to be improvements in the quality of the educational experience offered by the school, it was apparent that developments would have to be based upon existing strengths, rather than the immediate identification of weaknesses. Organisational change would only occur if the attitudes and perceptions of individuals could be influenced, and this would only be achieved through discussion and negotiation.

What, therefore, was about to be attempted, was an improvement in educational outcomes, through the personal and professional development of the people involved. Logically, this could only take place in an honest and open atmosphere, and through the appraisal of each member of staff including, eventually, the headteacher. Within a month of the writer taking office, the staff met together, and it was put to them that some immediate rationalisation of responsibilities was necessary. It was appreciated that if the effectiveness of the school as a whole was to be assessed, it would be necessary to evaluate each individual's contribution to it, and therefore job descriptions would have to be renegotiated.

Each member of the staff was asked to produce a confidential written statement of their present responsibilities, interests and areas to which they would like to contribute, and professional needs. It was emphasised that the main aim of this exercise was for the headteacher to get to know the staff better, and for there to be a basis for discussion in the initial professional development interviews. At no time were these discussions with staff to be referred to as appraisal interviews as, initially at least, this would have appeared too threatening.

The individual written responses varied greatly in length, but each produced information which made a positive contribution to the first series of professional interviews. Before these interviews took place, a possible match of people and responsibilities was drawn up, the relevant parts of which were to be discussed with each member of staff. Prior to this, discussions of initial observations and ideas had taken place with the deputy headteacher. Although she never read the staff's confidential written documents, it was important that the deputy should form part of the decision-making team from the beginning. The initial, individual meeting with staff, the first of a number of subsequent interviews, proved very worthwhile. Each lasted for approximately one hour and took place within school hours; the deputy headteacher being used to cover classes. The majority of the time in these first meetings was spent by the headteacher listening to an elaboration of issues which had been raised in the written document.

The interview was not a voluntary activity and there was some understandable unease. For some teachers, this appeared to be the first opportunity they had ever had to discuss their own professional interests and needs, and it was therefore welcomed by them. Others, however, were highly suspicious, only being prepared to respond to direct questions. It also became an opportunity for certain staff to bring their own personal agenda to the surface, by mentioning colleagues, and this had to be curtailed quickly. By the end of each interview, though, the appropriate area of responsibility had been raised and, without exception, the ideas put forward were considered positively by staff. After a few days for further consideration, each teacher returned, either to accept the new areas of responsibility, or to discuss specific issues in greater detail. For some colleagues the renegotiated areas represented a restructuring of existing responsibilities, with the emphasis being placed on curriculum co-ordination throughout the school, rather than within a single department. Other staff took on completely new areas; for example, moves were made from art and craft resources to library and information retrieval; from gymnastics and girls' games to language skills, although previous responsibilities were continued voluntarily here; and from stock control and requisition, to mathematics. These new responsibilities did not only involve teachers above Scale 1, as all staff had expressed a willingness to make additional contributions, and some Scale 1 teachers accepted responsibility for major curriculum areas, for example, science.

Job description

Following this stage, and still within the first two months of the new headship, actual job descriptions were negotiated with staff. These were based upon outlines suggested by the LEA, and were similar in expectation in so far as was realistic for each individual teacher. It was evident that the job descriptions would need to be altered and updated in the future, and so it seemed pointless to make demands of certain members of staff which they felt unable to fulfil.

Having reached agreement on the details of all responsibilities, criteria had been established upon which the staff performance and school development could be based. And so that everyone should understand the total situation, each job description was included in a booklet, which was given to every teacher, the school's governors and also to some of the local authority's advisers.

The job descriptions had outlined curricular responsibilities, which in many instances, would take considerable time to fulfil. It was necessary, therefore, to agree specific targets with staff, and also to place a time limit on these. Situation analyses were undertaken, and in the majority of cases, the first priority was to assess resources, discarding those which were obsolete.

The process of curriculum evaluation and renewal continued, despite progress during the following 18 months being hampered by the industrial action taken by the teacher associations. The inability to hold full staff meetings, made the discussion of curriculum matters very difficult, but the individual professional development interviews continued. These were still mainly concerned with the teacher's role as a curriculum consultant, with the targets set being short term, specific and usually easily achievable. Many staff were gaining considerable satisfaction from what was taking place, and from the feedback during their interviews. At this stage, however, basic attitudes, philosophies and classroom expertise were not being questioned, and so the discussions were still relatively non-threatening.

Staff profiles

In addition to the job descriptions which were produced, each teacher agreed to complete a *staff profile form*. There appeared to be little information available within the school regarding an individual's professional training, subsequent qualifications or INSET course attendance, and it was hoped, therefore, that the profile form would not only fulfil this need, but would also provide staff with a written statement of their own perception of their professional needs and career development. The forms contained sections relating to:

      (a)   qualifications including post-training;

(b)   present appointment and responsibilities;
(c)   previous teaching experience;
(d)   work experience outside of teaching;
(e)   professional development;
(f)   future plans.

The profiles were to be kept centrally, but were to be accessible for staff to update at any time.

The form itself was devised by the writer, as it was introduced during the period of industrial action when meetings were not possible. This lack of negotiation, was to prove a major weakness, as although staff agreed to complete it, and readily supplied factual details, the written response to professional needs and career developments was disappointing, with some teachers giving no information at all. Staff seemed to view the form as no more than a list of courses attended, and in the majority of cases, had to be reminded to update it; a task which was undertaken during subsequent professional development interviews.

Developing the appraisal structure

As the interviews have continued, over a period of three years, at the frequency of two per year for each teacher, they have altered in character. *The emphasis has moved away from evaluation of the role of curriculum consultant, to also encompass classroom expertise, professional and personal needs*.

This shift in structure, has moved the interview nearer to that of the industrial appraisal model, with its characteristics of: performance review; identification of areas in need of development; and the setting of specific targets.

To date, however, this is still being undertaken on a largely informal basis.

It had been the intention that as staff grew to accept and understand the positive benefits of professional development interviews, a more structured approach would be negotiated and implemented. It was envisaged that this would involve:

(a)   preparation, including a written statement of self-evaluation by each teacher;
(b)   classroom observation by the headteacher, based upon agreed criteria;
(c)   the appraisal interview itself;
(d)   a written agreed statement of outcomes and targets;

(e)   monitoring and follow-up action.

Although the climate for this development now seems favourable within the school, the advice given by the professional associations, for members not to co-operate in any pilot schemes involving staff appraisal, makes any new initiatives at this time inappropriate. This situation is not helped by the fact that the school is in one of the six local authorities participating in the pilot projects on staff appraisal techniques, funded by the Department of Education and Science. Any move would therefore be viewed as an LEA initiative, rather than a school-based strategy for improving staff development and educational outcomes. The time is not yet opportune to proceed and patience will have to be exercised.

Headteacher appraisal

It was mentioned earlier, that the appraisal system established, was not only to include each member of staff, but also the headteacher. This aspect of the appraisal structure came about through the writer's involvement in a pilot scheme within the LEA which considered headteacher appraisal based upon a headteacher-adviser partnership. The exercise undertaken, explored within a jointly agreed framework, the roles, relationships and skills involved when an approach to appraisal is carried out by a headteacher and a senior member of the LEA's advisory team.

The writer had been prepared to undertake such a venture, not only because of a personal interest in appraisal and the perceived benefits to the educational performance of the school, but also because of the possibility of enhancing the credibility of an appraisal system in the eyes of the staff. Furthermore, the views of the teaching staff on the performance of the headteacher were to make an important contribution to the final outcome of the appraisal.

It was agreed by the writer and the adviser, that before the appraisal exercise could take place, the role of the headteacher would have to be clarified. It was felt important that because this role was so complex, the actual appraisal should only focus on a selected range of key task areas. These would include not only the generic skills, basic to the role of all primary headteachers, but also contextual aspects, pertinent to the stage of development of the specific school.

If these contextual skills were to be appraised accurately, it was vital that the appraiser should be familiar with the school, its planned development and any constraining factors. This was to be achieved partly through the time spent by the adviser in observation, not only of the headteacher, but also within each class area. At the beginning of the exercise, the nature of the work being undertaken had been explained clearly to the staff, with emphasis being placed on the fact that the observation was a familiarisation procedure in order to appraise the headteacher's performance, not theirs. This aspect proved a threatening experience for some colleagues, although it did enhance the credibility of the adviser with others.

The involvement of the staff in the headteacher's appraisal was taken a step further, when it was agreed that their views could contribute an added dimension to the overall exercise. They were asked, therefore, to complete anonymously a questionnaire which had been devised jointly by the writer and the adviser, and which covered five contextual areas identified as important.

The areas selected to act as indicators of the headteacher's performance were:-

1. *Co-operation:* the methods used to facilitate and encourage class teachers to work together constructively.

2. *Motivation:* whether motivation and commitment within the school were linked to the headteacher's performance.

3. *Communication:* the nature and relevance of communication within the school.

4. *Links with outside agencies:* the different levels of involvement as related to the role of the headteacher.

5. *Control:* the determination and maintenance of policy, and the headteacher's awareness of the link between classroom practice and resultant pupil attainment.

These five key areas were explored by means of 14 questions, to which the staff were asked to respond. It was decided that the questionnaire should be a qualitative measure, involving written answers, which could be as brief or elaborate as the individual desired. This method was felt more appropriate than one based upon graded scales or ticking pre-determined responses, as it was hoped that it might elicit more open and informative replies

The actual questions included:

(a)   Do you find it easy or difficult to discuss educational matters with me? Either way say why you think this is the case.

(b)   Do you feel that you can influence developments in the
       school as a whole?
(c)   What are your views on how I handle conflict?
(d)   In what ways do you think I encourage teachers to work
       together?
(e)   Do you think you are kept informed about matters rele-
       vant to your work? If not please specify.

Of the total teaching staff, only one person chose not to be involved in
the exercise. When the writer saw the actual staff replies during the
analysis stage, they were completely anonymous, as the handwritten
questionnaires had been transcribed by the adviser. The responses
were honest and thoughtful and, in the majority of cases, very constructive. Many colleagues acknowledged the fact that they were
basing their perceptions on only two years of the writer's headship,
and that most of this had taken place within the period of industrial
action, when staff meetings were not being held. They were aware,
therefore, that some of their criticisms might be based upon the
situation, rather than the headteacher's style of leadership.
This particular approach, involving staff perceptions, was potentially
threatening, but in reality it formed a very useful element of the
appraisal procedure. It was possible to detect a definite pattern or
norm in the responses to a number of individual questions, and these
commonly held perceptions helped the writer re-assess developments
and future plans. Whether the statements made by the staff reflected
the actual situation was unimportant, what did matter was that if staff
perceived something to be a reality, it would influence their motivation
and co-operation.
The teaching staff's response to their involvement in their own headteacher's appraisal varied tremendously. Although never questioned
directly about this, it was possible to detect a number of differing
opinions:
(a)   they became involved because they were asked to by a
       senior member of the LEA advisory team;
(b)   the headteacher had only been involved to gain personal
       kudos and future promotion;
(c)   the headteacher's credibility rose and more credence
       was given to the changes that were being planned;
(d)   if the headteacher was prepared to be appraised, then
       staff appraisal was worthy of serious consideration by
       them.

It was this last view that the writer had hoped would emerge.

Future developments

Appraisal is surely the way forward to achieve an increased sense of professionalism within the teaching force, but there has to be preparation and it has to be introduced in a sensitive manner which acknowledges the legitimate fears of teachers. It can be argued that one method of introducing an appraisal system is for the headteacher's own appraisal to be undertaken before, or as an integral part of that of the teaching staff. For, having experienced some of the fears and anxieties, the headteacher should be in a better position to introduce staff appraisal in a more sympathetic manner.

So far, it has been a tentative step, but the responses and outcomes have been, in the main, positive. Staff have experienced the benefits of the professional development interviews and have seen some of the changes that have occurred in the areas of communication and decision-making since the writer's own appraisal. Now we await the right moment when we should be able to build on this base, and devise our own model for effective staff appraisal. One which, we hope, will not only improve educational outcomes, but which will meet the professional and personal needs of each individual teacher.

3.2 Staff Appraisal: a Tool for Performance and Professional Development

Peter Delaney

Introduction

In 1974, the Salford LEA invited a group of primary headteachers and advisers to form a working party to produce a document which would assist primary schools to review and evaluate curriculum, management and organisation. The result of our deliberations was *Salford Primary Profile*. This close professional involvement with institutional self-evaluation and a diploma course in education management led to a period of innovation at St Edmunds in which I attempted to integrate individual performance appraisal into the existing whole-school self-evaluation procedures.

At St Edmunds I had always attempted to develop a consultative ethos and encouraged the discussion of all issues fully and openly. During my research into appraisal it became increasingly obvious that the one aspect of the school we talked about less than others was ourselves – the most important resource available to our children. During the very early discussions on improving this situation, we all agreed that institutional self awareness and adaptability must be linked to a structured form of individual 'stock taking' of our own performance, progress, aspirations and prospects. It is useful to 'see ourselves as others see us' and there was a felt need to set aside time for observation and discussion of our professional practice on a one-to-one basis. Our long term plan was to integrate such a scheme into our existing management and organisational structures.

Purposes of appraisal at St Edmunds

The cornerstone of our scheme is the belief that teachers wish to improve their performance in order to enhance the education of children. To help staff in this process a school must reach agreement on how head and staff can best define the needs of individuals; how often this review should take place; how best can this be done; whether individuals can review their needs unassisted or whether they require help or guidelines; and, finally, how the head can best fulfil the responsibility for identifying and meeting the needs of the school and the professional development needs of the teachers.

The major gains could include more effective and productive professional liaison via mutual review and target setting; more systematic and frequent communication to facilitate agreement about performance standards and results; more explicit motivation by defining and clarifying key responsibilities; and, finally, a more detailed, realistic and pragmatic basis for team or corporate planning.

The emphasis would therefore be on development and shared perspectives with an acknowledgement by all concerned that there must be a state of readiness in the school in relation to curriculum management and administration. Means must be devised to collect, organise, use and record data produced by the system and the dialogue between teacher and head should reflect joint accountability and agreement on actions to improve performance.

We recognised that a joint approach to defining and resolving a teacher's development could create conflict between the teacher's expectations and the school's ability to deliver. One important advantage we identified, however, was that mutual problem solving could be presented in a constructive way rather than as a response to an inadvertently self-confessed need or crisis – fire prevention instead of fire fighting – with the teacher having the opportunity to share in the production and interpretation of the evidence as an active partner in the process. If the raising of educational standards is at the root of appraisal, the school must encourage increased levels of professionalism which require teachers to assume more responsibility for their own performance. It became apparent to us that self-analysis and appraisal must be built into the system. This process can become a working reality if teachers understand and believe in the results they are expected to achieve; if they are able to (or can be helped to) measure their achievements by an appropriate method of self-assessment; and if they have their achievements recognised and progress monitored on a regular basis. The head can help staff in performance analysis by sharing in efficient, open and regular review and, in doing so, help teachers to gain a clear idea of their performance in post and how this relates to the school as a whole.

School description

St Edmunds R.C. Primary School is a group 4 primary school in Salford LEA. It is situated in an outer suburb of the city, which was formally a division of the Lancashire LEA. It is a one form entry school, comprising a nursery unit, three infant and four junior classes. We have eight full-time teachers, one nursery nurse and myself. Areas covered by curriculum specialists include science, maths, computer technology, reading and language development, humanities, music and parental liaison. The school is organised in normal age bands.

Of the 230 on roll, two thirds live on a well-established council estate, one third live in private housing inside the parish boundaries. There are strong links between the school and the local community. Many of the parents were educated at the school and show great loyalty and support to all aspects of our provision. We have a well-established PTA.

Since the late 1970s we have had a stable staffing situation with the opportunities that that offers for social cohesion and the developing of shared perspectives. A high level of in-service activity and school-based debate and dialogue has characterised the school.

Scope of the scheme

The notion and possibility of a scheme of teacher appraisal at St Edmunds was first discussed informally with individual members of the staff. We also arranged formal staff meetings to discuss performance appraisal models outside education with the possibility of adapting aspects which could be tailored to the needs of a primary school. The main features of our own model to emerge were regular meetings with all teachers which took the form of carefully structured interviews, with these discussions being linked to regular informal and formal observation of teachers at work in their classrooms. My key tasks in the proposed system were to help the staff in critical and constructive job analysis and then to determine what action and resources were needed to improve job outcomes in class teaching and curriculum specialist roles.

Framework of the system at St Edmunds

1. *An agreed job description*

> (a)   class teaching
> (b)   curriculum consultant

2.   Element of formal and informal classroom observation
>   (a)   agreed criteria

3.   Regular meetings of individual teachers and head
>   (a)   agreed standards of performance in the classroom and specialist areas of the curriculum
>   (b)   joint setting of achievement targets
>   (c)   regular review and evaluation of performance and achievements

Description of the introduction of the scheme

From the beginning, in September 1981, all staff were involved in the discussions which led to the introduction of the scheme the following year. This section explains the sequence of these discussions and attempts to explain the rationale behind the processes and procedures we finally adopted in Autumn 1982.

Once it was accepted that the notion of an appraisal scheme was reasonable and professional, provided it had a developmental and supportive orientation, we had to decide what was relevant and useful to our school at that stage in its development and what would be acceptable to the staff as a whole. After an examination and analysis of our staff development programme and related management practices, we agreed it was essential to establish a set of pre-appraisal conditions in order to be organisationally 'ready' for the innovation. These included the regular and accepted involvement of the head-teacher in classroom activities; the continuation of staff meetings for school review and forward planning with the addition of regular developmental discussions or interviews between head and individual teachers; the revision of our jointly agreed aims and curriculum guidelines for the school, with a clearly stated, agreed and shared perception of the nature of effective teaching and classroom organisation; role descriptions for all members of staff (including the head); special documentation for individual review; schedules for self–appraisal and the production of a staff hand book on the appraisal system. The staff agreed that I should be the appraiser and, even though I did not have superior expertise in all aspects of the curriculum, it was agreed that I was the best person to carry out a general appraisal of their work and agree with them their needs for professional development. In most primary schools the head has the best knowledge of school context and climate and is able to take management action as a result of the appraisal since he or she is influential in providing in-service training and role changes within the school.

We gave much thought to the criteria and related qualities of our scheme. We concluded that it must provide genuine support to improve our provision; it must cover the full work of each teacher; the procedures must be clearly stated and understood; and its operation must not be cumbersome, complex, bureaucratic or time wasting. There was a general consensus that our scheme must place the emphasis on formative appraisal and that any criteria for successful performance must reflect the most important aspects of our work. Finally there must be a climate of trust and commitment to appraisal. These discussions did allay many of the fears of staff because it became clear that our scheme would not limit that degree of professional independence which they valued so much. Our aim was a high level of autonomy and self development.

The implications for the professional role of each teacher were examined at length. If appraisal is about professional growth, what are the implications for the school? Sharing judgements and feelings about job-related issues openly and honestly requires a school climate which is conducive to an open and trusting two-way dialogue. The staff and I agreed that this sharing and partnership would be more inviting if they knew *why* they are doing, *what* they are doing and *how well* they are doing it. Defined expectations, shared values, agreed purposes, known standards and positive feedback are all essential. Defining and sharpening job descriptions was our starting point, in relation to job purpose, content, key tasks and performance standards. The analysis of performance in class teaching and specialist roles requires relevant job blue prints. This sharper definition of the job would allow teachers and others to know on what basis the appraisal was to be conducted. Our job descriptions were framed to reflect the development of professional autonomy as well as the growing call for accountability. We attempted to develop a scale which effectively defined some of the qualities and skills which we considered important in classroom and extended professional activities. These criteria were elements that we considered make an effective teacher and reflect good practice and had to be established to aid our discussions on what contributes to effective performance.

One example of a teaching skills checklist is shown in Figure 4.

The curriculum consultants also needed a framework to assess their contribution to the school in general and colleagues in particular. The

Classroom Performance Criteria
RELATIONSHIPS
- Elicit and control children's response.
- Sympathetic knowledge of individual children.
- Established framework of expectations.
- Use of own interests to enthuse children.
- Good professional relationships with colleagues.

PROFESSIONAL SKILLS
- Understand schools aims and objectives.
- Sound theoretical base to classroom practice.
- Physical arrangements of room to support class organisation.
- Work matched to each child's stage of development.
- Selection of appropriate and relevant learning experience.
- Flexible grouping based on needs of curriculum and children.
- Efficient use of teaching space.
- Well organised and maintained equipment and resources.

EVALUATION
- Evaluation of classroom organisation.
- Appropriate records of children's progress and attainment.
- Planning records and forecasts for a balanced programme over time.

Figure 4 – Teaching skills checklist

basis of their appraisal would be curriculum planning and organisation, resource selection, collection and allocation, external and internal liaison, the formulation and monitoring of schemes of work and the promotion of in-service work.

It was then decided that our scheme should include both formal and informal classroom observation. The criteria we established for effective teaching were an essential prerequisite to any observation of teachers at work. We realised that there are obvious problems in evaluating classroom performance because a teacher has a relatively large degree of discretion over how the job is done. Despite this, we felt sure we could improve the objectivity of the evidence about job performance, by making it more relevant to job outcomes and taking into account actual behaviour and not inferred assumptions made at a distance. Our appraisal dialogue would use the *real* evidence of teaching skills. We felt that in the past we did not have a genuine forum for the exchange of ideas on teaching methodology and thereafter felt we would benefit by increasing our critical awareness of pedagogy. Schools about to introduce formal observation must consider: specific purposes; the status of the observer; the focus of the observation; duration and frequency; methods to be employed; documentation; appropriate criteria; use of evidence or outcomes; and post-observation forms of support. We decided on biannual observation, with prior arrangements with the teacher about the date and time of the visit and the type of lesson to be observed, using the 'teacher helper' mode of observation. Discussion of the criteria for the observation preceded the visit and I had access to the teachers' planning documentation. We decided that feedback should be given as soon as possible after the observation with a more detailed analysis at the appraisal discussion or interview. The nature and focus of this feedback is critical to the success of the observation. *The focus should be on: performance rather than personality; observations rather than assumptions, inferences or explanations; descriptions rather than judgments; the specific and concrete rather than the general and abstract; the present rather than the past.*

If developmental change and more effective teaching is to result from observation, headteachers must gain the support and co-operation of individual teachers and build in the vital elements of self-evaluation and self-improvement. The concentration must be on development, rather than on deficiencies, allied to a combination of feedback and performance analysis, which is the basis for professional problem-solving.We considered that our formal observation with agreed criteria, reflected my appreciation and the teachers' recognition of the centrality of the classroom in our school.

Our survey of models used in industry and commerce and my own research into industrial psychology convinced us that there was a place in the appraisal scheme for a regular discussion to provide feedback, exchange information and plan future actions. However, to integrate an appraisal interview into the existing communication and decision making procedures in our school was both complex and time consuming. I had to become fully conversant with the nature of interviewing, its purposes and objectives. Special documentation had to be prepared. The logistics of the interview had to be appropriate, with agreement about interview topics and sequence. Interview strategies, style, tactics and techniques had to be planned. The follow-up procedures adopted, including the completion of a report, which had to be agreed with staff in advance, because the interview stands or falls by the actions that result from it. The concept of bilateral commitment is central to the purpose of the discussion. The staff were especially determined that the actual discussion should be *structured* carefully so key parts of their jobs were covered in the reviewing and target setting process.

Interview structure: key topics

1. *Essentials of job.*

2. *Results achieved in past.*

3. *Set objectives for future.*

4. *Plan development.*

We designed self appraisal pro-formas to be completed by staff prior to the discussion. This documentation followed the planned and pre-arranged sequence of the interview.

Interview sequence

1. *Classroom observation. Summary discussion.*

2. *Classroom provision. Main targets for term.*

3. *Contribution to school.*

4. *Development plans.*

5. *School organisation.*

6. *Links with parents/outside agencies.*

We soon realised that we needed additional documentation to support the appraisal system in general and interview in particular. We devised a staff profile document which included general details and details of staff development.

Our fundamental belief was that the dialogue should be used as a tool for problem-finding not problem-solving. This is a more creative process, with a respect for and a knowledge of the various levels of competence on the staff. It became obvious that there is no single model for an appraisal discussion. Flexibility and an awareness of individual differences will improve feedback and encourage self appraisal, which is the ultimate aim when teachers are being helped to consider performance related problems and to take increasing levels of responsibility for their own performance. The process is one of partnership in which there is a clear understanding and acceptance of what the teacher will attempt to achieve and the degree of support and resourcing he or she will need. As a direct result of our experience we consider the following are important factors for successful appraisal interview outcomes: a highly participative problem-solving style with a past performance self-review by the teacher; open expression of feeling; non-judgemental approach by the head; criticism which is constructive and behaviourally related; and the feedback of specific information on positive achievements.

Summary and conclusions

The scheme we introduced in Autumn 1982, and was fully operational until the advent of the recent industrial action. The main components of the scheme remained unaltered from 1982-1986. During that period however we did extend and improve the self-appraisal questionnaires which were used by staff and head prior to the appraisal interview. This element of self-analysis was helpful to teachers who were attempting to set their own standards, monitor their own progress and provide their own feedback. The role of the head in this performance analysis and development is critical. Fellow headteachers will have to appreciate that successful introduction will make demands on their knowledge and expertise in classroom teaching because, quite naturally, staff will expect headteachers to possess the professional qualities and skill which they are working towards. *Appraisal cannot stand alone as a management aid. Performance and professional development are the prime considerations with appraisal as a consequential and contributory element.* Its value and success will always be in proportion to the skill with which the headteacher uses it. This, of course, has training implications. The higher the skill level the more effective the system. Although it was a major innovation at St Edmunds and a significant management task, we had at all times to retain a sense of proportion, otherwise the tail may have wagged the dog and we may have taken on a system which has a habit of taking on a life of its own. The Chinese compare running an organisation to cooking a small fish. It should not be overdone. Appraisal is not a substitute for management and should not be elevated to a position of overwhelming importance whereby it is seen as the only organisational means which is critical to improving the work of the teachers and the school. *As a management tool with acknowledged limitations it should be integrated into existing management and organisational structures. Appraisal is not an 'optional extra'. It should be an inextricable part of effective management*. Our belief at St Edmunds is that the main consequence of development appraisal will be the generation of an expectation of change in teacher beliefs and practice and in the organisation of their schools and curricula.

CURRENT APPRAISAL PRACTICE : SECONDARY SCHOOLS

3.3   Appraisal at Altwood School

Roy Taylor

Introduction

Altwood School is a suburban 11-18 mixed comprehensive school of 900+ pupils, with an 'open entry' sixth form of about 110 students. It was formed in the early 1970s, firstly by the merger of two 11-16 single-sex modern schools, and then in 1973 by its change-over to an 11-18 comprehensive school.

The catchment area provides a very wide social mix and children come from urban, suburban and rural areas, many from large private and council housing estates.

The school is organised academically into eight faculties – each with its own teaching area(s) – and there is a horizontal pastoral system with a head of year (and assistant) for year 1, years 2 and 3, years 4 and 5, years 6 and 7.

Several of the staff at middle management level taught in the secondary modern schools. Many of those who were appointed expressly for the change-over to a comprehensive have now been promoted outside the county. It has been found that the in-service training given to them by the school places them in a very good position when applying for promotion.

The younger staff fall into two categories – they are either unmarried or are married but without parental responsibility. The cost of housing in the area militates very strongly against teachers being able to survive on one income, therefore many staff are forced to commute into school. Many of the married female staff are part-timers and, together with some of the full-time members of staff, have young children at primary school. This can affect attendance at after-school meetings.

Historical background

In 1978, two senior teacher posts became available at the school and one of these was given to the head of science to be professional tutor, a role previously undertaken by one of the deputy heads as part of his job specification.Early in 1979, prior to the retirement of the head-teacher, it was felt by many at senior and middle management level, who already had job specifications for their roles within the school, that a useful way of updating information on all teaching staff would be to ask for a revised curriculum vitae. This curriculum vitae would also contain information about what courses each member of staff had recently attended and what extra-curricular activities they were involved in, both within education and also outside the school. Although some might have seen this as an accountability exercise, others saw it as a useful way of encouraging professional development once individual needs had been identified.

In May 1979, during the term prior to the arrival of the new head-teacher, the professional tutor compiled a list of areas that the staff thought it would be helpful to include in a staff appraisal form, incorporating the best from current methods used within and outside education. This form for middle management was arranged under four general headings:

1.   academic/pastoral commitment of the head of faculty/year (including strengths and weaknesses, organisation of meetings, etc);

2.   general competence and leadership – completion of tasks, delegation of responsibility, selection of staff, evaluation of work;

3.   qualities of character and personality (including sensitivity to others, behaviour in stress situations, career ambitions, etc);

4.   qualities of intellect and attitudes in certain areas – new ideas, problem-solving, changing of entrenched ideas.

In the first instance, members of the middle management team were appraised by two of the three deputy heads: the completed appraisal form was given to the appropriate head of faculty or year for comment and amendment or alteration where necessary. Having agreed together on the contents of the appraisal form, both parties signed it. It was then kept safely in a central place by the professional tutor, but *not* with the individual teacher's personal record file.

Each head of faculty and year then prepared an appraisal report on each of the members of their faculty or year team, using the same four general headings and adopting the same methodology as had been used for them. An unstructured interview was held with individual members of staff if there were any problems. It was stressed to the staff that the whole purpose of the appraisal form was to help the professional tutor in his work.

Many of the staff had been appointed to the school either before it went comprehensive or in the first few years of it becoming comprehensive and, because of relationships built up over the years, saw nothing threatening in either self-appraisal or appraisal by another colleague.

In September 1979, the new headteacher joined the school. At his previous school (where he had also been headteacher), he had held annual 'staff development conversations' with each member of his staff. This general interest of his provided a necessary ingredient for continuing the previous scheme, but encouraging more areas of interest.

In 1980, a two-page structured form, entitled 'Staff Appraisal Check', was compiled by the professional tutor and issued to all staff during the early part of the summer term, prior to the appraisal interview. The actual interview was a new ingredient in the appraisal exercise. The form gave a fuller opportunity for voluntary self-appraisal and evaluation by the appraisee prior to the interview. The completed and signed forms were passed to the headteacher who, after reading them, extracted general comments and ideas for action or further discussion, needs of individual teachers, and ideas for school-based in-service training. He then produced a general report for staff and notes for the professional tutor, containing discussion papers and agenda items for further discussion.

In a few cases, follow-up interviews were held where it was felt necessary to discuss the professional development of individual staff. In no instance was any report shown to, or discussed, either with other staff or anyone outside the school without prior permission being obtained.

The following year, the previous years' appraisal form was returned to the individual teacher prior to the next appraisal. This report could be kept or destroyed at that teacher's discretion.

Aims and purposes

A scheme of staff appraisal should have clear aims and objectives. The Altwood scheme is founded on a supportive approach i.e. it aims to encourage teachers to develop their full potential and to work towards a greater degree of common purpose within the school. *It is both retrospective (a review of past work) and prospective (majoring on career development)*: it gives the individual teachers an opportunity to assess their own work and look at their own professional and career development, as well as affording an opportunity for guidance and advice where necessary. Some of the objectives of a staff appraisal scheme will aid teachers and improve their performance as teachers, their morale and their communication whilst other objectives will aid the general management of the school by using staff potential and interests.

Staff perceptions of the scheme

As might be expected, staff perceptions varied from the very critical – 'it's a check', 'it is a provider of information – to be used at a later date' – to the very positive – 'it helps me to review positively both my failures and successes'. At least one member of staff saw it as a useful way of providing an opportunity to air grievances. However, the majority of staff – at all levels of responsibility and with differing lengths of service at the school – saw it as a positive review of the previous year's work, where areas of need could be diagnosed and stimuli could be given to improve performance. It also could be a useful aide-memoire of what had been undertaken in the various areas of staff and professional development.

The scope of the scheme

The format

Because the appraisal scheme started as an exercise between senior and middle management, it was seen by staff on Scales 1 and 2 as something which management not only talked about, but participated in, and were prepared to act upon the results of the exercise. They also saw it as something which could be beneficial in a variety of ways – and so were prepared to take part themselves. It still is, after eight years, a voluntary exercise and in different years, depending on pressures on middle management at the time, has a varying percentage of staff participating. The pilot scheme, referred to previously, was a useful introduction to a more specific form of staff appraisal. If that had not been undertaken, the climate may not have been judged right at that point in the school's history and, therefore, there could have been resistance to it. *If staff appraisal is seen to be imposed by senior management without due care, thought and attention being given to it, it can be seen as something to cause a rift between the headteacher and his or her staff.*

Schools undertake staff appraisal with varying degrees of formality and structure. Structure and form can set appropriate boundaries to work within and from which one can expand. However, it is felt by some that the opportunity to develop strengths and minimise weaknesses could not take place in such a structured situation. Conversely, if a more open approach were adopted, although a wide variety of issues could be covered, unpalatable issues could be avoided.

The interview

The interview is seen as a key part of the appraisal. It is often the only time in the year when two people can find the time to sit down and have a systematic discussion about what they do and the effect it has on those they teach. A skilful interviewer will help the interviewee to identify strengths and weaknesses and examine ways of building on the first and eliminating the second. The nature of the interview will vary considerably – depending on whether the interviewer can offer support and encouragement for good practice and be able and willing to grapple with less successful aspects of work, and work constructively for improvement.

At Altwood, the dual system of interviews allows every member of staff to be interviewed at least once, giving the opportunity for each class teacher to have the two strands of their work appraised in a positive way and each head of faculty to have their pastoral work appraised, and each head of year, senior teacher and deputy head to have their academic work appraised. It is interesting to note that it is common for pastoral and tutorial problems to surface in an academic or subject interview, and vice versa: comments and concern about the general running of the school surface in either or both interviews. However, there are problems that have to be faced in any interview scheme: the interviewee's superior may not be considered by the interviewee as an acceptable person to carry out an appraisal interview. In such cases a second person has been found who is acceptable.

Another problem that occurs if the appraisal scheme involves the same people year after year is that the same discussion can occur on each occasion and so the scope for change becomes less and less. Here again, the opportunity has been given to staff to ask for one of the senior management team to act as interviewer.

The fact that some of the senior management team had attended courses on interviewing techniques as used both within and outside education, enabled them to compile a four-page handout entitled 'Notes on Conducting the Appraisal Interview', which dealt with such topics as preparation, planning, techniques to use, and follow-up. In summary – **be prepared, be positive, be professional, be yourself!**

The annual report

Some of the information obtained at the interview often becomes incorporated in the annual report of the appropriate faculty or year head four months later. None of this information is of a confidential nature – in fact most of this information is about what individual members of staff have been doing both within and outside their faculty or year team, e.g. their involvement in extra-curricular activities, participation in in-service training, new initiatives being planned or undertaken, etc. An outline of the interrelation of appraisal interviews and annual reports is given below (Figure 5).

Classroom observation

Classroom observation is a common feature in schools, particularly those that have teaching practice students or probationer teachers. Part-time teachers and new teachers sometimes are observed in the classroom situation. However, this observation has often been seen as a subjective exercise, regardless of whether a detailed checklist or open-ended questions are used. The same may be said of classroom observation of other staff. In some faculties and year groups, interest

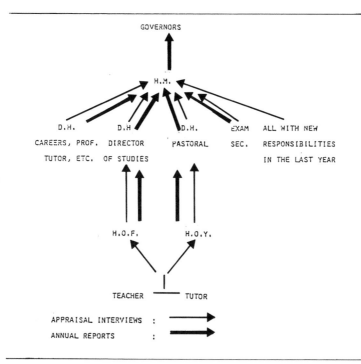

Figure 5 – Interrelation of appraisal interviews and annual reports

in classroom observation has been shown and in two faculties some experimentation has been undertaken.

There are several prerequisites for any classroom observation – especially if in the future it is to form part of a statutory staff appraisal scheme. ***Discussion with the teacher concerned, both before and after the observation, is essential***. The discussion before the observation should lay down the ground rules so that both the appraisee knows what is happening and the appraiser is given some pre-knowledge of the planned lesson. The discussion after the observation should be a constructive and co-operative review of the lesson, aiming to praise good practice and looking for ways to minimise poor practice and eliminate problems. In order to record correctly what was said in the post-observation discussion, a written report should be given as soon as possible afterwards. One danger of lesson observation and appraisal is that it may focus on the teacher's behaviour, whereas the real issue is whether or not the pupils are learning and reinforcing those attitudes and patterns of behaviour implicit in 'education for life'.

The staff appraisal scheme described and analysed

Decision-making processes

Over a period of years, there has evolved in the school a form of collegiate responsibility, with each head of faculty or year being allowed a certain amount of autonomy, but responsible to the head-teacher, who is seen more as a team leader, who manages resources. The faculty and year teams are far more of a cohesive unit, working for the good of the school, rather than for their own good.

The senior management team of seven meets every morning for a quarter of an hour, before school begins, and also once a week after school for an hour. The head and deputies also meet once a week for an hour; the heads of year are timetabled to meet once a week in school time, under the leadership of one of the senior teachers; the heads of faculty meet twice a term with one of the deputy heads acting as chairman. Year teams and faculty teams meet twice a term. The middle and senior management teams (designated the Monday meeting) meet together after school for an hour twice a term.

The timetabled structure of these meetings is such that matters of general school policy can be aired at the senior management team meeting, then discussed at the Monday meeting, before proceeding to faculty or year level, prior to further discussion, either by a full staff meeting or further discussion at senior management level. Before implementation of any major issue, the reports from groups within the staff are considered and as many avenues as possible are explored. A final document is then formulated for dissemination and application. Both pastoral and academic areas are carefully monitored by the three deputy heads; as members of individual teams, they are able to keep au fait with feelings at grass-roots level.

Appraisal methodology

Mention has already been made of the self-appraisal exercise prior to interview, the interview itself and the various methods of follow-up. Although the completion of the whole exercise involves a lot of extra time and energy, the majority of the staff, which now has a somewhat different make-up from when the appraisal system was introduced in 1979, find it a meaningful exercise. Some 22 of the staff (40%), mainly in middle and senior management positions, are still at the school, and the majority of them will probably stay in the same or similar positions until they retire.

Some concern has been expressed as to why the pastoral aspect of the staff's work is also appraised. This is seen as a vital part of a pupil's development as a person, in spite of the fact that in some circles in the outside world, academic results are the only criteria by which a young person is assessed. A pupil's 'education for life' is very important and if the school can assist in that process as well, then methods of tutor work need to be regularly appraised, in order that only the best takes place.

Problem areas

When the first major staff appraisal check was published, some difficulties in wording were discovered, especially those that dealt with strengths and weaknesses. Some class teachers felt that if they asked for help in certain areas, this may be interpreted as a sign of incompetence, whereas it was originally intended that if staff were finding problems in certain teaching groups, assistance should be given to that teacher and specialist training to help overcome such problems. Yet when 50% of the staff were asked 12 months later if they knew why the wording on the second page had been changed, they were unable to say!

Many members of year teams thought, rightly or wrongly, that their head of year knew all about them and so this appraisal exercise was, at the most, an opportunity for them to receive 'a pat on the back' in a pleasant atmosphere. One or two of the staff thought that the questions should have been more detailed and less general – 'it lacked specifics' – therefore it could be deemed to be superficial and therefore of limited value to the interviewer.

Results

On the negative side, one third of the staff commenting on the whole exercise saw it as having no personal benefit for them at all – the majority of these were female teachers who had been at the school for a number of years and were now well into their teaching career and feeling that they had reached their promotion limit.

Very few of the staff saw how any aspect of a staff appraisal exercise could bring them out of fairly tightly knit faculty or department teams into a cross-disciplinary group working for the good of the school. In fact, few teachers at that time, 1981, saw how staff appraisal could be of any benefit to the school. Fortunately, such views are rarely held or even voiced six years later.

Heads of department, who met their head of faculty on a regular basis and discussed curriculum matters with them, did not find the academic interview of much value. Since that date (1981) it has given an opportunity to discuss related issues far more deeply, and whereas in the early days of appraisal many staff did not find the appraisal form a useful way of monitoring either faculty or department progress, nowadays assessment as a form of monitoring is far more commonplace and in some cases can be traced back to appraisal in its early days.

On the positive side, nearly all staff valued an opportunity to talk to at least one person for a limited amount of time to take stock, set targets and, most importantly, plan personal career progression. The interview also seemed to provide greater mutual understanding.

The written report compiled after the interview was seen by many of the staff as a valuable method of setting targets for the next year and making suggestions for professional development. Initially, the fear that reports would be seen by others or could be used in a negative way against them was a fear expressed by some staff but this has completely disappeared.

The majority of staff were satisfied with their teaching commitment: during the years, several teachers had been able to extend their teaching expertise into other areas within their main subject, and others had the opportunity of teaching their second subject. Other staff who would have liked to alter their teaching commitment now understood the reasons why it was difficult to do so after the timetable had been constructed – perhaps the way of obviating this would be to have the staff appraisal earlier in the academic year.

The appraisal interviews have highlighted how many members of staff were either giving or willing to give of their expertise outside their own subject discipline to help pupils – especially those studying for external examinations.

Many members of staff now saw that the interview was a useful and positive way of monitoring progress and several, including two long-serving teachers, had found it a useful way of restructuring priorities. Several staff also saw the interview as a useful way of suggesting new ideas for implementation within their own particular faculty (perhaps they felt that if their ideas were noted down, somebody would have to act on them).

Summary

Progression since 1983

In 1983 the form – now renamed 'Staff Appraisal Interview' – was subdivided into two main areas: academic and pastoral, on separate sheets of paper, with a space by each subsection for the interviewer's comments after completion of the self-appraisal by the appraisee and interview with the appraiser. Part of the feedback now included a personal reply to each member of staff.

Up to 1984, nearly all the staff participated. With the advent of teacher unrest late in 1984, participation in 1985 and 1986 decreased considerably, in spite of the fact that in 1986 it was renamed 'Career Development Discussion'. In 1987, the staff appraisal is still voluntary: however there is a rider that if any member of staff was unwilling to take part, the matter should be discussed with the headteacher.

In 1984, a meeting for appraisers was held and some profitable discussion took place. It had been hoped that a meeting in 1985 would major on interview methodology, but this did not take place. Feedback and outcomes of the appraisal were two important items highlighted in the 1984 discussion.

Perceived objectives

There were several objectives of the process that were perceived by staff, e.g. a clearer understanding of the school's aims and objectives. On the professional development side, staff were now identifying and clarifying In-service training needs and career aspirations, and many staff had an increased awareness of potential for either promotion or change of role. On a personal basis, the review of the previous year's work had a positive effect as it was seen to give support for good practice and success: the setting of targets for the coming year and planning of work were now also major features of the scheme. There were also far more improved relationships with immediate superiors.

Results

As a result of some of the issues raised in the 1980 appraisal, a weekend staff conference took place in 1981: one of the major issues discussed was the role and place of active tutorial work. Since that date, a far more comprehensive and cohesive programme of personal and social education has been undertaken. In the year 1981-1983, several INSET meetings after school and a weekend conference at the local teachers' centre were funded by the LEA, with outside expertise being used in a positive way.

As a result of the GRIST proposals – areas of school staff development highlighted in appraisal became the basis for development – a do-it-yourself career development group has been formed and a course for middle management has been run at the local teachers' centre, with LEA funding and using external expertise.

Several curriculum development initiatives have been undertaken, both within the school and also with outside help.

At middle management level in the school, there have been several instances of job rotation within the pastoral team, and within faculties there have also been some instances of role change. Other staff have been willing to revise their career progression strategy. In the year 1985-1986, seven members of staff left for promotion and three members of staff were on secondment.

The headteacher felt that he knew individual members of staff better and was able to delegate and deploy staff far easier: he also felt that the appraisal forms did allow him the opportunity to gauge the staff's feelings and to let the staff have the opportunity to let their own feelings be gauged on various issues.

Within the actual day-to-day context of teaching, there were now improved teaching styles, improved lesson content and, in some cases, improved relationships with classes. There have been changes in the allocation of teaching groups and rooms. Some staff had been given opportunities to widen their experience by teaching different subjects or classes. Certain areas of school life had been carefully studied by working parties as a result of identification in appraisal, e.g. detention, homework policy.

Upward assessment

It is often assumed that the only method of appraisal is downward. One head of faculty at the school has experimented with a system whereby his faculty staff appraise him by analysing his work at middle management level on a checklist, with each item graded on a five-point scale (Diffey 1985).

Conclusion

Prior to the initiation of a staff appraisal scheme, certain groundwork needs to be covered. It would seem that four essential items would be:

1. a clear understanding of the aims, objectives and boundaries of such a scheme;

2. confidence by as many parties as possible that the scheme has value;

3. an interview structure that allows both parties to cover specific areas and answer specific questions adequately;

4. a written report with clearly designated guidelines for usage and time lengths for retention.

The first appraisal at the school came at a time when relationships and trust between senior and middle management and general classroom teachers, had been built up positively over a period of years. If this had not been so, the exercise could have been a disastrous failure.

It should always be remembered that if any interview is perceived as having an effect on salary, promotion or status, it will produce very different responses to one which is structured towards professional development and a review of positive performance.

If a staff appraisal scheme is badly thought out, clumsily implemented and cumbersome to operate, it will almost certainly do more harm than good.

3.4 The Introduction of a Staff Appraisal and Development Scheme into a Large Comprehensive School

Michael Valleley

Introduction

Knutsford County High School was established in 1973 by amalgamating boys' and girls' secondary modern schools which served the town. Prior to that time when Cheshire had selective education, the children who passed the 11 + examination received their education in Wilmslow, Macclesfield or Manchester.

Knutsford itself has a population of 14,000 and is conveniently situated 20 miles south of Manchester within easy access of the airport. It has many interesting historical aspects. The name is supposed to have come from Canutes Ford. In more recent times the architect, Richard Harding Watt, designed many Italianate buildings for the wealthy merchants of Manchester. These are now a feature of the town, merging comfortably into a mixture of architectural styles including a fair amount of black and white framed houses with thatched roofs.

This environment being so close to Manchester is an attractive residential area for commuters but some major employers – Barclays, National Nuclear Corporation and Ilfords – have purchased large manor houses and developed their grounds to form attractive working environments for their employees. The town is therefore largely a middle class town, with an overspill estate built on its perimeter providing the school with a socially divided catchment.

In 1981 when the appraisal scheme was first considered, the school was a Group 13, 11-19 comprehensive of 1,800 pupils, 230 in the sixth form and a special education centre which catered for 42. It is a split-site school, the lower school being half a mile away from the upper school. The leisure and recreation centre facilities are shared with the community. The youth service has a base within the buildings, and it is an adult education centre with extensive community letting.

The need for a staff development scheme

When I became the headteacher in January 1981, the school had been well founded on comprehensive lines, was beginning to achieve academic respectability and was known for its progressive curriculum. Whilst there was cross-curricular discussion, I was concerned about the geographical isolation of departments and the scarcity of normal staff discussion as there was no staffroom large enough to hold all staff. In such a widespread school on two sites, communication is an obvious problem and the added absence of any system of staff records provided a situation which was fertile for the growth of a staff development scheme.

The teaching staff at the time numbered more than 90 and were an interesting blend of youth and experience. Specialist staff were available to teach all subjects and the majority of these were fairly recent appointments making the staff rather younger than the average for a school of this type. At the time they were considering pupil assessment in its widest form. I was a newly appointed head who knew no-one and had only minimal information for confidentials and was attempting to get to know a huge number of new personalities. One of the cross-curricular groupings looking at pupil assessment suggested that it might be an idea to consider the staff as well as the students; from this suggestion staff development grew into a school issue. This received fairly widespread support from staff and an in-house conference was arranged to discuss the issues. Perceived school needs were identified by means of a questionnaire completed by all staff and this provided the starting point for the conference. An outside speaker from a major commercial organisation was invited to give his views on appraisal and development and to outline the way this was carried out in his organisation and the importance which the company attached to this scheme. The afternoon sessions of the conference concentrated on the possibility of introducing a school-based model of staff appraisal and development.

As a result, the recommendation of the in-house conference, a sub-committee was appointed which represented wide interests on the staff and all levels of seniority, including myself.

The brief given to this sub-committee covered six areas. These were:

1. that the climate should be 'right' and that there should be benefit for the individual and for the institution;

2. that the scheme was to have regularity, probably an annual scheme, and probably largely conducted during the summer term;

3. that the scheme should be operated by the head and the deputies although there was to be investigation of middle management control and even peer group appraisal;

4. that it was considered important that self-appraisal formed part of the scheme although the availability of this assessment to anyone other than the individual was the subject of much concern;

5. that the confidentiality of the whole scheme was to be an important factor, but this was to include accessibility for the individual;

6. the final area of the brief was that there should be explicit reference to certain areas particularly actual teaching, departmental and staff relationships, total contribution to the school, new skills and individual input as well as personal ambition.

The sub-committee met on several occasions and reported back to the full policy committee, which is made up of senior management, heads of department and heads of year. Although the subject caused great discussion on all levels within the staff and not least in the policy committee itself there was a considerable amount of agreement about the scheme proposed. The reference to schemes of appraisal in industry which covered many of the major national and international firms represented in the northwest made us aware of the pitfalls of confusing performance and potential and it was agreed that emphasis must be given to the important individual contributions which were made within a successful institution and that these should be recognised irrespective of the potential for advancement within the profession either internally or in another educational institution.

The areas which were the greatest cause for concern among the staff were committing professional views on colleagues to writing instead of talking to a head or deputy about them. Several members of the middle management were worried about this issue. Another factor which caused concern, evoked considerable discussion and at the time required most delicate handling, was the confidentiality of the material produced by the scheme. This was finally agreed when I stated that I considered that ultimately this material was the property of the individual member of staff and that the only keys to the filing cabinet in which it was kept would be held by myself and my secretary who would be instructed not to release any file without my expressed permission. It was appreciated by staff that a deputy head involved in an appraisal interview would need to have such access.

The scheme devised by the sub-committee has been subject to only minor modifications. Probably the major difference is that, on the pilot scheme, the self-assessment forms were the property of the individual member of staff and were only used by them in preparation for their interview – a practice which was changed early in the pilot scheme.

The policy committee recommended that the proposed scheme should be put to the whole staff and run as a pilot study, and that unless an individual chose to opt out of certain parts of the scheme, that it should be considered a whole school initiative.

The scheme

The scheme adopted broke down into three areas of assessment: self-assessment; assessment by an immediate superior – a head of department or a head of year; and the interview with a senior manager – the head or deputy head. These three stages would then be fed into a teacher's file accessible only to that teacher and the head.

The self-assessment form

The self-assessment form concentrated on three areas: current strengths and needs; career interests; and developmental needs.

In considering current strengths and needs, attention was drawn to classroom, pastoral or extra-curricular involvement which provided job satisfaction. The objectives which had been individually set for the year were then to be considered, as were key skills and areas of strength which were utilised or not, in the teacher's present situation.

When considering career interests the member of staff was asked to be realistic about career ambitions both in the long and short term.

In the third section, an expression of developmental needs was required which firstly identified how lack of appropriate skills, knowledge, qualifications or experience had limited progress. Resulting from this and taking a slightly wider view, a developmental programme could be suggested. And, finally, any change in personal considerations such as mobility or lack of it, was requested.

Direct appraisal

The second stage of the scheme was the direct appraisal by the head of year or head of department on the individual's performance during the preceding year. Each member of staff received a departmental and a year report. These commented on the contribution made in administration, relationships with other staff, relationships with pupils, classroom management, contributions to teamwork, extra-curricular activities, and any other factors.

These reports when compiled were shown by the head of department/ head of year to the individual member of staff who had an opportunity to discuss them in an interview situation and also to complete their own comment section which was part of both forms.

The self-appraisal form together with the departmental report and the year report, form the basis of the agenda for the interview between the head or deputy which was the next stage in the scheme.

Interview

The starting point for most interviews was likely to be how well the previous year's objectives had been achieved; the factors which had prevented progress; or in some cases made it possible to achieve more than had been thought. The interviewers who had received no training whatsoever had to be aware of the necessity for listening skills and a counselling approach, irrespective of their normal personal style, if the interview was to be of value to the interviewee. Whilst there was no flexibility possible regarding the immediate manager (i.e. head of department/head of year) at the interview level, it was possible to allocate a particular interviewer for a particular interviewee, but in the vast majority of cases departments were interviewed so that an interviewer could gain an overall view as well as an individual one.

Following the interview a brief report was written which included comments on: present situation and performance; career ambitions and potential; and developmental needs, as well as any other important factors which had arisen during the discussion. This report was shown to the interviewee who was encouraged to comment verbally and in written form if he or she so wished.

The teacher's file would therefore contain self-assessment, appraisal by head of department/head of year which included reference to classroom performance, and the interview report written by a senior manager. Members of staff were invited to also include any other information which they felt might be a useful record of their contribution or achievements. The restricted accessibility of this file to the head and member of staff concerned was considered to be of particular importance.

Benefits of the scheme

It was considered that the scheme should provide individual and institutional benefits. For the teacher, it was intended to enhance personal performance by setting new targets; identifying needs and finding remedies for those needs; to identify and enhance career opportunities; and in a very large school, to provide access to senior management. The benefits for the management would be the creation and maintenance of an up-to-date record of performance, improved communications and the identification of school needs. The institution should benefit from an improved performance on the part of its staff with the possibility of building higher morale and better team consciousness. In practice, the staff proved most willing to produce frank, well-balanced self-assessments which identified their achievements, their failings and their targets. The only suspicion was from a small number of the longer serving teachers or the less secure. The second stage, the head of department and head of year assessment, was welcomed by this middle management group as a good opportunity for the formalisation of the relationship between colleagues. However, this stage could be considered to be a weak link: the reports tend to concentrate on positive aspects and either exclude or deal too briefly with areas of weakness which may be the most important areas for development.

There is a marked difference in frankness between the self- assessment and the manager's assessment. The day-to-day contact between the participants may be a contributory factor to these reports being sometimes closer to 'references' than 'appraisal'.

A survey conducted among the staff showed that they valued the interview considerably. *The opportunity of contact with senior management was appreciated and the head and deputies found the feedback valuable but not always painless*. It was possible to set useful targets and identify needs as a result of the interview not only for courses and in-service training, but also for two-way observation within the school and other educational institutions. *It provides a major opportunity for the head or deputies to recognise the amount of good work being contributed by all members of staff*. There is a danger of mutual admiration rather than frank discussion taking place but the major problem is that of time. The interview is vitally important to the member of staff concerned and cannot be rushed. This process when repeated for every single member of staff is extremely time consuming.

The teacher's file produced provides excellent documentation for the head and the individual member of staff. There is a danger that the process stops in the filing cabinet and that co-ordination of INSET needs does not take place.

Appraisal of headteacher

Whilst I support appraisal for everyone, I have not been successful in providing this for myself. The feedback from the interviews in my direction is considerable. I also receive a certain amount of information about my performance from my deputies, students, parents, the school's general adviser, the district education officer, the chairman of governors and secondary head colleagues. There have been suggestions and even experiments using retired headteachers as assessors. The pace of current developments in education seems to increase daily and it must be questionable as to how long these colleagues will remain sufficiently in touch to be able to carry out a satisfactory appraisal of the situation. Another attempt has been the grouping of heads so that they may help evaluate each other's performance. Pressure of work coupled with major changes in role would make heads unlikely to have the time or the inclination to leave their own schools to attempt to identify the minute as well as the obvious differences in another educational institution.

Conclusion

The appraisal scheme at Knutsford High School was at a crossroads. The time had arrived for an internal review and the choice would have been to continue with the existing scheme or, more likely, to propose a modification. However, the national initiatives proposed by the Secretary of State and the effect this will have on local authorities in the formulation of alternative schemes, may well affect such decisions. One thing is certain, however, and this is that the willingness of the staff to participate in the scheme at a time of professional uncertainty, the mutual benefits gained by themselves and the school, and the experience which we have had of operating such a scheme within the institution, can only be of advantage whatever the future may hold.

CURRENT APPRAISAL PRACTICE: COLLEGES

3.5 Annual Review – a Staff Development and Counselling Model

John Jennings

Introduction

The 'annual review' system at Barnet College was introduced and operated in some departments in 1982 and all colleagues were able to participate in 1983. This case study will attempt to outline how the scheme was introduced and into what sort of existing institutional climate. The initial and developing staff perceptions of the review in operation will be discussed. An attempt will be made to make an assessment of the pitfalls and limitations as well as the possible benefits, both institutional and individual, of such a scheme.

Background

Barnet College is the larger of two colleges of further education in the outer London borough of Barnet. It currently has an establishment of 208 FTE teaching staff of whom 167 are full-time appointments. The college is now based on two sites about three miles apart although for most of the case study period it was based on one main site with some peripheral accommodation. For administrative and management purposes the college is divided into five large departments described as faculties. In this case study the single term 'department' will be used rather than 'faculty' and material has been edited where necessary. Additionally the term is used in the further education sense and involves responsibility for between 30 and 40 academic staff. An increasingly important role is now designated to course-based boards of study. The work of the college is broadly tailored to its mainly residential and commercial catchment area. There is little local manufacturing industry.

The student body is recruited locally and from neighbouring London boroughs and Hertfordshire. In total there are 1,200 full-time and some 8,000 part-time students. The students represent a variety of ethnic and cultural backgrounds.

The teaching staff of the college is a mix of those with long service or experience and those new to the college or to teaching. Staff turnover has been relatively high in the past five years, many colleagues having taken advantage of the availability of the local authority's premature retirement scheme. All sections and levels within the college adhere to this pattern of change and over forty percent of the present academic staff have joined the college since 1982.

Staff development within the college is the allocated responsibility of the principal. The staff development programme is managed by a small staff development management group and the staff development sub-committee of the academic board. The full-time professional tutor is a member of both groups and is a key member of staff in the delivery of staff development activities. His present involvement includes: induction, counselling, organisation of in-house training, and dissemination of external courses. He also monitors the annual staff review process.

Developing the scheme

At Barnet College, the idea of a 'personal review' resulted from the introduction of the concept of staff development into the college. In 1981, when this initiative was begun, very little in the way of staff development activity existed apart from attendance at in-service Cert. Ed (FE) courses. Attendance at short courses was minimal and visits to the FE Staff College at Coombe Lodge rare. There was no in-house or course-based activity or organised support for colleagues joining the college. In addition, in the college there was a serious rift between 'management' and a large section of the teaching staff as a result of a dispute over regrading which had attracted national publicity and national union support.

The catalyst and initiator of the introduction process was a new vice-principal, it may be critical to have such an outsider to highlight the need for change.

The process adopted made use of the existing consultative machinery and resulted in the formation of an academic board staff development working party.

The composition of this working party was an important factor in achieving a final report which married the requirements of the college management and of the teaching staff as a whole, but challenged the fixed perceptions of both.

At Barnet the working party, chaired by the vice-principal, included representatives of all levels of the college hierarchy, importantly the 'managers' were in a minority with respect to the 'managed' and the latter had therefore to acknowledge ownership of the final package.

The report which was accepted by the academic board began with a short statement of the college staff development policy. There then followed proposals to support the aims of the policy: for a continuing staff development sub-committee, for 'personal review', for the induction of new colleagues, for monitoring and delineating promotions, and for a professional tutor in the college.

The five elements of the policy were:

1. to encourage job satisfaction, personal achievement, individual and team effort, and thus provide for personal advancement within the college or outside it;

2. to develop staff in ways which will help to maintain and improve the overall effectiveness of the college in meeting the vocational, general educational and leisure needs of the community;

3. to help colleagues to maintain and improve teaching skills and methods, particularly in the light of changing educational and personal needs;

4. to marry where possible the interests and needs of the individual and the department or college;

5. to ensure all colleagues have an opportunity for development through the operation of an explicit and systematic process.

And the first step to implement this policy should be that there should be a systematic and continuous, personal review which should comprise:

(a)   personal discussion, at least annually, between each colleague and their head of department;

(b)   provision for the exchange of items for discussion, beforehand, in order to facilitate the dialogue;

(c)   a properly documented record of the appraisal discussion, with both the head of department and the colleague retaining a copy of the statement as agreed;

(d)   with the agreement of the head of department and the colleague, the professional tutor could be invited to attend the discussion;

(e)   the record of the discussion should constitute a basis for developmental action by the head of department and/or professional tutor;

(f)   by drawing together the needs of individual colleagues, the head of department should present a profile of the staff development needs of the department which would be presented to the staff development sub-committee of the academic board annually.

Before describing the practice and progress of the scheme, it is probably useful to observe that the initial concept was of 'personal review' but that the term 'appraisal discussion' was also used in the staff development policy statement. Although this phraseology was made less acceptable after Sir Keith Joseph suggested tentative links between pay and appraisal, the element of measuring or assessment is included in our review process. It may be surprising that a broadly based working party agreed with these ideas. It was, the writer suspects, partly as a defensive mechanism in the college atmosphere at the time which as noted above was divisive with management being given little credibility and trust.

Personal review was seen as an opportunity to put down and record markers for an individual, and this was eventually supported by the introduction of an open reference policy in the college. A final initial comment is that on practical grounds the format that developed was review on an annual basis, thus 'annual review' has become the existing usage rather than 'personal review'.

As it stands our scheme does not include a mandatory element of classroom observation although it is not ruled out. An attempt to increase the chance of such observation taking place was made some two years ago but the college staff development committee felt unable to proceed. As far as is known colleagues have not requested such a formal inspection.

The writer's view would be to agree observation in principle, but the mechanics of such observation needs careful thought.

The annual review system is attempting to support all colleagues and it is difficult to see how one or two short visits are going to help the 75-80% of colleagues falling into the competent/good band. The writer feels strongly that the poor/marginal performer is not to be helped within this framework but needs support as soon as difficulty is identified.

As a way of increasing teaching competence, team teaching, 'open' classrooms and sharing of materials and experience may have greater potential for success as well as being less threatening.

Monitoring and evaluation

The professional tutor evaluated the 'annual review' process. Initially this was done by talking through with all the heads their perceptions of the review and in the following year by relatively lengthy discussions with a cross section of colleagues, all of whom it so happened had had reviews.

From the latter discussions, which took place after the third round of reviews, it was possible to identify strengths and weaknesses in the perception and practice of reviews. Shortcomings were identified in the practice of both the reviewers and the reviewed as well as positive attitudes and procedures. A written report was subsequently discussed with heads of department and by the staff development committee.

In general, colleagues saw that benefits could result from participation; indeed they perceived that the generation of positive outcomes was essential for the long-term health of the review process. They recognised the need to improve the status of the review, to make it special and distinct from other contacts or discussions during the year. In some cases there would be a need for more continuous review. It was also important not to discourage heads of department from having an interest in the work of colleagues throughout the year. The voluntary nature of the review should remain, although as managers, heads of department might more actively engineer the setting up of reviews. Compulsory reviews can easily prove ineffective if the reviewed refuses to participate actively. This is equally true of voluntary reviews undertaken as an easy option to refusal.

Many colleagues clearly had little conception of the format of a review. This was particularly evident in the reported length of some of the reviews. Length does not equate with quality although it may equate with thoroughness. No minimum time can be mandatory as the very reluctant participant may be determined to terminate the review as quickly as possible. Only a skilled and experienced reviewer might counter such tactics. However it would seem that little can be achieved in a review lasting half an hour. Indeed discussions about reviews were often double this length. Apart from reluctance to participate, short reviews may indicate a mutual lack of general or particular preparation for the review and a lack of skill in developing and drawing out attitudes and perceptions in discussion.

After the initial round of reviews it had been thought necessary to provide pro formas (Jennings and Skitt 1987) to provide an information base for the discussion. Many colleagues saw a benefit in updating their head of department on their past year's activities and addition or updating of qualification or skills. It was an incentive for some to keep an organised record of what they had done and was thought useful in the preparation of job applications.

A few colleagues felt that committing themselves in the sections of the pro formas concerned with future patterns of work and career development was exposing and unacceptable. The anticipated perception of the review being a two-way exchange of ideas, without prejudice and in an atmosphere of trust, was clearly not fulfilled for these colleagues. However heads of department rarely gave advance notice of particular topics for discussion. With or without the use of the pro formas, some colleagues admitted that they had not prepared themselves effectively for the review discussion. One identified the inadequacies of his review after attending external interviews. It was suggested that the head of department needed to be able to fulfil the role of a helpful reflective participant.

In their assessment of their reviewers, colleagues thought it necessary that all heads of department should have a sound grassroots picture of the work of individual colleagues and should develop a 'presence' in all sections of the department. The writer would add to this the willingness of the reviewer to spend time establishing a colleague's contribution to the work of a department possibly by adding enquiring skills to listening skills. Some colleagues suggested that some other person might be more appropriate than the head of department but the alternative reviewer was not clearly identified.

Colleagues were asked questions about the style and content of the review. Most colleagues thought that their review had been conducted in a friendly manner with little associated stress. Some suggested that it was difficult to achieve a genuine two-way exchange of views avoiding a reviewed/reviewer or boss/worker stance. Although avoiding tension, many reviews were considered not sufficiently businesslike. A serious professional discussion was required and it was appreciated that this might be more questioning and demanding of the participants. The content was often disappointingly narrow, often linked to the possibility of promotion rather than the generally more possible personal development in terms of career variation and individual satisfaction. In exploring their perceptions of their reviews with colleagues many side issues were raised, most of these topics could properly have been explored as part of the 'annual review' itself.

The staff development policy clearly highlights the need for adequate recording of the review discussions. This was a task which had been found difficult and in some cases records had not been produced. Two problems were identified. What is the style and content of the record and how is it obtained? Often the record was thought to be a reasonable and true record of the review but limited by the content of the review discussion. Agreed records were thought to be bland in nature, relating the areas explored but not sufficiently precise in identifying areas of future progress or commitment. It was thus difficult to use them as a reference point for change and, with the passage of time, the exact meaning was rapidly eroded. The mechanics of production of the review record concerned some colleagues. A conflict existed between the need to maintain confidentiality and the desire for a typescript record. A possible solution is for the reviewer to produce the draft and final record on a word processor. It would be unfortunate if freedom of discussion was limited by perceptions about the security of the recording process.

From the review record two parallel ways forward are identified, one on an individual basis and the other on a collective basis as a 'departmental profile of staff development needs'. A review should in most cases identify some outcome or agenda for action and this should form part of the agreed record. It may identify a need for material provision, course attendance, or a change in teaching or administrative responsibility. It was seen as critical that agreed aims should be followed up between reviews. This was a joint responsibility, although either party might have the task of initiating action on any individual item.

It is worth emphasising that not all needs can be met and that objectives must be realistic. The 'departmental profile of staff development needs' was not directly a subject of discussion in the evaluation although it is probably worth noting that comments on the individual records apply in part to the profiles and they tended to be written in very broad terms. In this form they were difficult to use as the basis of planning future staff development activity.

All the colleagues approached had had at least one review. Some were doubtful that they would participate next time. Three reasons were identified: lack of effectiveness or content in a previous review;

lack of delivery of items identified in the review; and loss of personal confidence in the head as a reviewer.

As a result of these discussions the process needed to be made more effective. Firstly there was a need to amplify and reinforce the general level of colleagues' information and expectations of their 'annual review'. Colleagues should know what to expect and what they had a right to expect from the head of department. There was a need to support the heads of department by offering and organising skills training in reviewing. Conversely, as participants, colleagues had a duty to prepare themselves for the review by some form of personal or self-review.

After discussions and consultation with the heads and the staff development committee, these objectives were tackled in the following ways. A small group wrote further notes for guidance (Appendix A) and the discussion of reviews in the induction programme for colleagues joining the college was reinforced. Secondly, heads of department, if they were to retain their major responsibility for reviews, needed support in developing their skills. This was a difficult matter and progress was only possible when a new principal was appointed. Then, a two-day residential skills workshop was organised using external tutors with positive results. My perception would be that if a broadly counselling model of 'annual review' is attempted then the skills of those primarily responsible must be checked through and reinforced. A head of department may not have well developed listening and counselling skills and although we might seek them in future appointments there are inevitably competing attributes and experience which might be considered more critical in selection for a particular post.

Provision for senior staff

The scheme as presently formulated, clearly identifies the head of department as one party to the review and a more junior colleague as the other participant. What is the procedure for more senior staff up to and including the principal? This has varied and developed during the operation of the scheme. The present pattern is that the principal would expect to review individually the senior management team, that is the heads of department, vice principal and two senior administrative officers, as well as the professional tutor. The principal has sought and obtained review from a 'review panel' of members from the senior management team and separately by the professional tutor.

Additionally each review carried out, if it is a genuine two-way exchange of ideas and perceptions, enables the manager to build up a picture of his or her effectiveness and image.

Present development

It is still recognised by most colleagues that a review carried out effectively is a beneficial process and that all colleagues should feel able to participate. A significant minority of colleagues in the 1986 round of reviews did not take up the option of having a review and alternatives to the established pattern were considered by the staff development sub-committee. As an interim procedure for 1987 the senior management team agreed that if requested they would carry out a review of colleagues for whom they were not directly responsible. Some colleagues have taken up this offer and have had reviews. Some others have had extended discussions with the professional tutor within a similar format to that suggested for a review.

Further consideration will be given to widening the choice of reviewer. This must involve principal and senior lecturers and would potentially involve some 20 extra colleagues in the role. If adopted, this mechanism would require rethinking of the mechanism for obtaining a global picture of staff needs. The perceptions and experiences of individual heads, which have made them unacceptable in the review situation to some colleagues, would also apply to this new cohort of reviewers. The need for training would be equally valid and they would need to be willing volunteers. It would also be necessary to provide time for them to participate in reviews since a colleague seen as a 'good reviewer' might attract a considerable clientele but unfortunately not in a quantitative and predictable way.

A further factor in our continuing review of the annual review process is the requirement to demonstrate clear mechanisms for identifying individual staff development needs in submissions for funding under Grant Related In-Service Training – GRIST. Here, well constructed departmental profiles of staff development needs are valuable and guidance has been given (Appendix B). To complete their picture, heads may have to ask individual colleagues to discuss staff development needs as a single item and in a more mechanistic way as an alternative to a full review. It is believed there are wider benefits in the 'full' annual review scheme, and that the truncated, essentially compulsory alternative would be a poor second-best.

Learning from experience

Using our experience at Barnet, I would give the following pointers to institutions embarking on the same road:

1. Decide the model of review that you are wishing to adopt and what is the purpose of the exercise.

2. Decide who, with training, will be able to manage the procedure as reviewers.

3. Acknowledge the workload required if the process is to be effective.

4. Ensure that adequate recording and feedback mechanisms exist.

5. Ensure that a match exists between the agreed outcomes and provision both financial and institutional.

6. To achieve the above, involve a broad spectrum of colleagues so that the scheme is their's and not the management's.

Appendix A: annual staff reviews – notes for guidance

Preamble

The purpose of the 'notes for guidance' is to assist in continuing to improve the quality of the review process.

1. The review is, and should be, distinguished from other contacts and discussion between head of department and a colleague which continue throughout a year. The review does not replace a continuing dialogue or relationship, although it may underpin and strengthen it.

2. The process, therefore, requires forethought and preparation by the participants. Where possible, the participants should arrange the review two/three weeks in advance.

3. In view of the delicate yet substantial nature of the process, it is recommended that only one such meeting is planned for a morning or afternoon with the possibility of follow-up meetings.

4. It may be helpful for participants to exchange beforehand, a written list of issues for discussion. For example, issues might include:
    –   present pattern of work
    –   further variation in work/new teaching
    –   information about the work area or curriculum design areas
    –   colleagues' perception about their own development
    –   colleagues' role within the department, team, college
    –   relationships
    –   information updating (pro formas 501 and 502 are available)
    –   forms of assistance/support for training and development

5. Some colleagues may wish to prepare for their review either by informal discussion with the professional tutor or a proximate colleague.

6. The professional tutor may, of course, be present at the review at the request of the member of staff or at the head of department's request, with the member of staff's agreement.

7. A clear structure and sense of purpose should be created, whichever style is adopted. It is for the participants to agree how

the review should be conducted. Some will prefer a more formal, others a more relaxed style.

8. The participants should conduct the review without prejudice and it should reflect mutual respect and confidence in each other. Participants should be sensitive to the fact that it may be necessary to re-establish or improve confidence and respect.

9. Brief notes made during the review would facilitate the process of subsequently producing an agreed record. Where possible, participants should formulate their interpretation of the record at the end of the review or immediately afterwards.

10. The agreed record will invariably contain proposals to be carried through by one or both participants. The record should make explicit ways in which follow up is monitored and implemented.

11. Where a colleague declines to have a review, both the head of department and the colleague should consider why that is the position. Should they choose to do so it may be useful for the colleague concerned to discuss their position with another senior colleague or the professional tutor.

NOVEMBER 1985

Appendix B: Departmental staff development profiles

The staff development committee makes the following comments about the general nature and content of the 1985/6 departmental staff development profiles.

The staff development policy indicates that these profiles are primarily derived from, summarise and co-ordinate needs arising from the individual staff reviews.

Most of the 1985/86 profiles do not fully achieve this target and thus provide a basis for planning the staff development programme.

A departmental profile is not intended to be a departmental report although it might be appropriate to preface a profile with such a section.

A departmental profile is not the arena for general staffing or management concerns to be expressed.

A departmental profile should be sufficiently detailed for a positive response to be made in terms of the area concerned and the type and extent of provision needed.

It may not always be appropriate to identify individuals by name, but some indication of the number of staff involved enables a correct choice of in-house or external action.

Recommendations

The next round of department profiles should contain a designated set of elements. An initial checklist would be:

1.   A short general introduction.

2.   A statement on the current participation in the review process and comparison with previous year(s).

3.   A description of identified needs. This has to be in three sections:
      (a)   Needs relating to departmental groups or course teams;
      (b)   Needs relating individuals or small groups of staff
      (c)   Specific individual training or support required.

It would seem likely that:
      (a)   would be met by in-house provision.
      (b)   would be met by a combination of external or internal courses (possibly depending on inter-departmental aggregation of needs).
      (c)   is likely to result in external course attendance, secondment or individual tuition and support within the college.

4.   An indication of future longer term needs and changes in provision within the department with staff development implications.

5.   A summary of any departmental or course team review which has been undertaken during the period covered by the review.

At some stage it might be necessary to consider profiles compiled on a board of study rather than a departmental basis.

NOVEMBER 1986.

3.6 Swansea College: the Introduction of a Staff Development/ Review Process

Guy Danhieux and Brian Robinson

Introduction

The purpose of this chapter is to describe the establishment of a staff development and appraisal policy in a new tertiary college. The policy developed in two stages; firstly as a relatively short-term process to meet the requirements of setting up the college and secondly as a long term policy to meet the needs of the staff and the institution in a rapidly changing educational environment. This discussion concentrates on the latter stage, but it is also necessary to understand something of the background.

Background

Swansea Tertiary College opened in September 1985 on the site of Swansea College of Further Education, which it replaced. The new college has 130 staff and approximately 1,200 full-time and 3,000 part-time students. West Glamorgan County Council's policy is to establish a tertiary system throughout the county – there are now four tertiary colleges – but sixth forms still survive and in fact there are two large comprehensive schools within a mile of the campus.

Tertiary organisation has had a profound effect on the college. It had been a very traditional institution, both in outlook and organisation. There were 80 staff (the vast majority of whom had been at the college for many years) organised in a typically hierarchical departmental structure. Into this stable atmosphere came sudden and significant change.

A new principal was appointed in September 1984, and within a month the LEA had decided to bring tertiary reorganisation forward by a year. The timescale had suddenly been halved, and this produced enormous pressures. There was now less than a year to establish a new college structure, agree staff re-deployment from schools, appoint new staff, develop the curriculum, establish proper liaison procedures with the partner schools, etc; all this whilst also negotiating and then coping with the effects of a £4 million building programme which would allow proper facilities on one site rather than being spread over three.

The new structure introduced in September 1985 was a functional matrix. Two vice-principals (academic and resources) were appointed and five directors (studies, student affairs, resources, development and personnel). The staff were organised on the basis of common areas of work into 12 sections.

One of the most significant lessons learned from this experience was the crucial importance of allowing a proper timescale for change. A major educational reorganisation causes upheaval and uncertainty for all those involved. So much happens so quickly and people find many of the changes potentially threatening. Discussion was truncated because of pressures of time, and because people were unclear about what was happening or why, a smooth transition became much more difficult. A planned staff development programme to allow a proper induction programme for staff of the new college (and that meant everyone) was simply not possible. Final staff appointments, including some at senior level, were not made until May 1985, and so the first full contact with some lecturers was not until the college actually opened. There was a proper induction programme for these staff in September and probably the most valuable item both for them and for the other staff was the production of a comprehensive staff handbook. This detailed the aims and objectives of the college, administrative procedures and the detailed job responsibilities, from the vice-principal downwards.

Setting up the system

The new academic board, in its first term, set up a staff development sub-committee with the following remit:

1. to establish a college policy to satisfy the needs of TRIST and the grant-related arrangements post-1987;

2. to establish the means by which staff development needs are recognised;

3. to plan and organise in-service training within the college through seminars and specialist inputs;

4. to promote the induction of new staff or staff filling new roles;

5. to recognise how expertise gained by recipients of staff development can be transferred to other staff.

The committee was chaired by the vice-principal (resources) but he shared the main responsibility for this area with the director of personnel. The committee comprised staff representing different sections of the college, but at first representation was not complete.

Both the vice-principal and the director had very clear ideas about the organisation of staff development and appraisal. *Firstly and fundamentally, it could not be something imposed by management on the staff*. To do so would simply generate suspicion, and as already indicated, this was one of the prices paid for the rapidity of the reorganisation. The policy had to come from the staff themselves. The role of the senior management team was to encourage and facilitate this process.

Secondly, staff development should be curriculum-led. Colleges are concerned with organising effective learning situations and it is the staff who are closest to the demands of the curriculum who are also most aware of their needs. The main unit for staff development is therefore the course team.

Thirdly, there should be no shying away from the issue of appraisal, but it must be clearly understood what the college means by the term. This was of great importance because the programme followed shortly after Sir Keith Joseph publicly indicated that he saw appraisal as a mechanism for removing weak staff from teaching – with the obvious union reaction. It was made very clear that as far as the college was concerned, appraisal had nothing to do with this kind of 'hard' approach of a top-down policy to determine necessary sanctions (up to and including dismissal). Sir Keith was also describing evaluation or assessment – i.e. carried out by one person on another – whereas appraisal is a two-way process. He was concerned with discipline, and it was stressed that the college's staff development/appraisal policy had nothing to do with this. There were clearly laid-down disciplinary procedures in existence and these should be used if appropriate. The college's policy was concerned with 'soft' appraisal; a supportive, counselling process, to identify needs and agree methods to meet these. Appraisal is a positive process, concerned with generating improvement.

Fourthly, there was a need for the gradual growth of a staff development/appraisal policy, rather than an attempt to devise a fully-fledged scheme. There was a belief in a bottom-up, curriculum-led system which should be seen to be coming from the staff and not from senior management. The policy evolved as staff saw its benefits and the committee suggested improvements. It was important that the committee reported to academic board meetings and not to management meetings. In fact, the policy has never been formally discussed by the management team. Staff discussion was encouraged and channels of communication to the committee were made clear and effective.

There were some advantages in policy development. Outside funding via TRIST meant that it was possible to plan some INSET programmes which were felt to be of particular importance without turning to the county for help. This was important at the beginning because it rapidly became clear that if the committee was going to function effectively, it was in need of some staff development itself. Procedures in the old college had probably not been unlike many other institutions; people applied for courses which appealed to them and if they had their head of department's support, the form went to the authority for approval – and if it was rejected an explanation was rarely given. Little analysis of need took place and certainly there was no structured development programme; and in fact, there was little understanding of the term. The first priority was therefore an INSET programme for the committee – partly in-house and partly bringing in external lecturers. This was done after the committee had identified what they felt their needs to be; an example of practising what was being preached.

It took the committee approximately six months to devise its staff development policy and get its approval by academic board so that implementation could begin. Two basic strands were identified through which the policy was to work, the first being, as has already been mentioned, the course team. (In the case of GCE work the emphasis is on the subject team.) Each course and subject team was to generate a 2-3 year plan of perceived need for staff development, reflecting all the factors which impinge on their work. This plan should be with the director of personnel at the beginning of each academic year, and he worked with the course tutors and subject leaders to effect a planned and co-ordinated programme via:

      (a)   in-house course team workshops;

(b)   in-house training using expertise from other areas of the college;

(c)   use of appropriate courses promoted by outside agencies.

A diagrammatic version of this process, indicating some of the major influences on course team planning is indicated in Figure 6:

The second strand, which is of equal importance, is the development needs of individual members of staff and it is this strand which leads

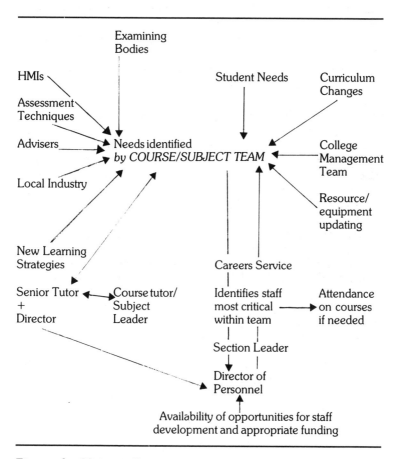

Figure 6 – Major influences on course team planning

into staff appraisal. One advantage was that developments in national policy – TRIST and then GRIST funding – and in our LEA meant that there was college control over spending (i.e. if it was decided to do something, it could be delivered) and a clearly defined budget. This meant that there was credibility; the committee was not simply going to be a talking shop with no clout. This process was helped by the attitude of the principal who made it clear right from the beginning that he would not interfere with the committee and would give his support to its decisions. This was crucial if the policy of 'bottom-up' staff development was to have any real meaning.

In 1986, while the committee was still at its earliest developmental stages, the LEA, responding to proposed GRIST funding, asked each member of staff and each course team to fill in a pro forma, indicating perceived development needs for the next year. This was organised by the director of personnel, with completion being voluntary. The result was a return of 70%, and this was collated by the director and established college priority areas for staff development. The committee then planned the programme for 1986/87 and staff were therefore able to see a clear correlation between their statement of need and the priorities to which support was given.

At this stage it began to be appreciated just how important the work of the committee was becoming. Because the college controlled its own staff development budget, lecturers' requests for INSET no longer disappeared into the LEA's administration with a positive or a negative result coming (eventually) from the heart of a bureaucratic system. Each request now went to the committee and it was decided upon, or, to be more precise, it advised the principal as to whether or not support should be given – but, as already indicated, the principal has always supported the recommendation. Gradually, the committee began to evolve more sophisticated systems to allow it to make a judgement on full information. The frequency of committee meetings increased; lecturers were encouraged to put in written briefs in support of their requests. Eventually, the committee decided that it would have to alter its representation to ensure that every section of the college was represented. It wrote to each of the 12 sections and asked them to nominate a representative, laying emphasis on the commitments this would involve – not just of time but also a willingness to take the responsibility for presenting the problems of dealing with disappointed staff.

Major issues

The new committee then addressed itself directly to the issue of appraisal. The decision to use the term was crucial. It has already been indicated that simply to impose a full appraisal system from cold would have been counter-productive and everything that has so far been described is an essential background to the next step. It was agreed that the impersonal mechanism of form filling to allow individuals and course teams to identify their development needs was not sufficient and a more pro-active process was required. Every member of staff is grouped in a section and the section leader is responsible for them. It was therefore logical to bring the section leaders into this process and for them to have review meetings with each member of their staff. As this idea was developed in the committee, concerns were raised about four main areas:

(a)   the format of the review;
(b)   whether or not it was to be compulsory;
(c)   its confidentiality;
(d)   the qualifications of section leaders to carry out the task.

A great deal of appraisal documentation was collected which has been produced in other colleges. An attempt was made to identify those elements which would best suit the college and what it was trying to do. After many attempts and much re-drafting, three documents were produced which it was felt would suit the purpose. It was stressed that these were open to amendment in the light of experience. The first document was an invitation to the member of staff (from his or her section leader) to come to a review discussion at an agreed time and date. It asked the member of staff to think about their experience over the past year and to consider future intentions. A 'buzz' list of questions was used to do this. Some days notice was given so that each lecturer had sufficient time to think through what was to be discussed. The second document was for the section leader, to give a checklist of the major items to be covered in the review. The third sheet was an agreed record. From the discussion, the section leader and the member of staff were to produce a record covering the main areas of the discussion, and recording any action which was to be taken as a result. This record would need to be mutually agreed. A copy of each of these documents is given in the Appendix.

The question of compulsion caused great debate. If it was voluntary, some people – possibly those in greatest need – would refuse the review; and if it was the case that this process was a crucial part of staff development then it was hardly consistent to make it voluntary. However, if it was compulsory, should staff have a choice as to with whom they had their review? Section leaders know their staff best and have direct responsibility for many areas, e.g. timetabling, resource allocation, etc, which are of major concern to staff. But there are personality clashes, etc, and in these circumstances it was suggested that staff could opt for a review with the director of personnel. This seemed too soft an option. *If the review was a positive, supportive process for the benefit of staff, and relationships had deteriorated to such a point that a lecturer could not have such a conversation with his or her section leader then this was an issue which had to be faced, not avoided. It was eventually decided that if these circumstances arose the director of personnel would see the two individuals together and discuss the problem with them – i.e. force them to face up to the issue.*

There was clear concern about how confidential the agreed record would be. Eventually it was agreed that only three copies would be created. One would be lodged with the director of personnel as he had overall responsibility for the programme, but this was purely a central file and no-one else would have access. The other copies would belong to the section leader and the member of staff. Confidentiality could be broken only with their joint agreement. For example, if the review identified action which required the involvement or consent of a third party, then obviously that person would have to be involved. This was acceptable to everyone.

Interview skills training

A review/appraisal discussion is not an easy process to carry out; it is a skill, and if it is important, it must be ensured that section leaders are properly qualified to carry it out. Training is not cheap, but fortunately the college is part of an All Welsh Staff Development Programme funded by MSC, and they were willing to fund a training programme for section leaders. It was considered important to go to outsiders for two reasons. First, specialist trainers were wanted who could offer a defined package in interviewing skills. Second, by being willing to pay for training, it was demonstrated to the whole college how important the review process was felt to be.

However, this decision had its dangers; if everyone was appraised, who would appraise the section leaders? This had to be senior management. Was it being suggested that they did not need training, but that section leaders did? This could be divisive, and so it was agreed that the outside providers would initially train the senior management team, who would then carry out the review with section leaders. This process again stressed the importance of the review for the whole college and gave the section leaders experience of being appraisees before they became appraisers. Their training programme lasted two days and at the end a review was carried out with the section leaders and some minor changes in the review documentation were made. At this point a very practical problem was dealt with: where were the reviews to take place? It was necessary to guarantee privacy and no interruptions, and so half a dozen rooms were identified and a booking system developed, so that rooms could be reserved. One advantage of holding the formal review meetings after Whitsuntide was that, because of examinations, it was the one time of year when rooms are available.

A meeting with the section leaders was arranged for a week later, when each would have carried out at least one review, to discuss any problems which may have arisen. Without exception the section leaders were pleased with the favourable response they had received. Staff were reacting positively to the opportunity to discuss their needs and many had spent a long time preparing for the review; copious notes were much in evidence.

This was obviously very reassuring for the section leaders and the committee. Staff were showing a willingness to take part and were perceiving the review as a positive process. In the Whitsuntide period teaching loads were at their lightest and this, plus the availability of interview rooms, meant that section leaders could complete their reviews by the end of term. The greatest number for an individual to undertake was 14.

An agreed review and action plan is clearly only part of the process; it identifies need and that is valuable, but the validity of the exercise is greatly reduced if no apparent action results. As has already been explained, some areas of change identified in the review can be dealt with by the section leader, others he or she must agree with the appraisee to refer on for discussion and action. It is crucial that staff are kept fully aware of what is happening. They are much more likely to accept a negative response to a suggestion if they have been properly involved in the discussion.

The sum of all the individual reviews plus requests from course teams is collated by the director of personnel and used to provide the basis of the staff development programme for the following year. Next year section leaders and staff will review how the agreed goals have been achieved. Although the formal interview will be a central part of this, appraisal review should be going on informally throughout the year.

Conclusion

This chapter has dealt with the origins and implementation of the college's staff development/appraisal policy up to the present time.

The response so far from staff has been very positive and advice to any institution thinking of establishing a formal review/appraisal system can be summed up as follows:

1.   Do not impose from above. The initiative may well have to come from senior management, and obviously they must be prepared to support the policy and its implications; but a programme that comes from the staff themselves is more likely to meet both their needs and their approval.

2.   Allow sufficient time for proper discussion to take place. Appraisal is a word which worries people and if they feel they are being rushed into a system which they do not properly understand, they will be hostile.

3.   Do not try a pilot scheme. If your argument is that a review system is of great importance, how can some people be left out?

4.   Do not be afraid to ask. Many colleges have tried, with varying degrees of success, to introduce appraisal systems and are very willing to talk about the pitfalls they faced. A great deal of literature has been produced and reading this will save re-inventing the wheel. There are experts available; our outside trainers were excellent – and we also gained a lot from discussions with the Further Education Staff College.

5.   Be prepared to spend money on training. Interviewing is a skill and too many mistakes are already being made in the education service on the assumption that because an individual has reached a certain level of management, he will automatically make a good interviewer.

6.   Finally – and possibly of greatest importance – go for a system which suits your institution's individual needs, i.e. the most comfortable fit. Complex formal systems may look wonderful on paper, but if the staff do not like them, they will not work.

Appendix – Documentation

Annual Staff Review

The review is intended to be focused on four key areas.

(i)   *Past year's work*

    e.g.   What has given you the greatest satisfaction?
What are your preferred courses/subjects?
If you are a course tutor – difficulties in carrying out this role satisfactorily?
If there have been obstacles which hindered you in accomplishing what you would have wished, are they likely to recur?
Has communication between you, your colleagues, the section and the college generally been satisfactory?

(ii)   *Improvements*

    e.g.   In order to improve your job performance, what changes might be made by:
(a)   Management?
(b)   Yourself?
(c)   Anyone else?

(iii)   *Development programme for the next twelve months*

    e.g.   What would you like to teach?
What activities would offer you more experience (e.g. course co-ordinator, school liaison, counselling unit etc)?
Are there any specialist training/courses which you wish to follow?
Have you skills/abilities which you feel are not being used to advantage within your sphere of work?

(vi)   *Career*

  e.g. What are your career objectives:
      (a) generally?
      (b) within the institution?

What help could the college give you in achieving these?

Check list for members of staff

You will shortly be invited to a discussion with ....on ....
at............ in...........at which we will be able to discuss your work
experience over the past year and consider together a development
programme for the next year.

To help us to gain most from this opportunity you are asked to read
this form and give some thought to the following points:

1.   How clear are you about your major duties and responsibilities?

2.   During the past year which aspects of your work have you most
     enjoyed or which have given you the most satisfaction?

3.   What do you feel you have done least well or has given you least
     satisfaction?

4.   Have there been any obstacles or hindrances to your work
     during the past year? Have you any suggestions as to how these
     might be overcome?

5.   Are you undertaking any aspect of your work – academic or
     pastoral – without understanding the reason for doing it? What
     do you need explained and by whom?

6.   Have you skills or abilities which you feel are not being used to
     advantage within your work?

7.   What would you like to achieve in your work during the next
     year?

8.   How do you see your career developing over:
     (a)   the next year?
     (b)   the next five years?

9.   Is there any area of work in which you think extra training or
     experience would improve your present performance or pre-
     pare you for your career development?

PLEASE ALLOW AT LEAST ONE HOUR FOR THIS DISCUSSION

	Aspect	*Observations*	*Action*

1.   Past Year's Work

    (a) Most satisfaction

    (b) Preferred subjects

    (c) Course tutor role

    (d) Obstacles

    (e) Communication

    (f) Unused/underusedabilities/skills

    (g) Other

2.   Development Programme for 1987/8

    (a) Teaching programme

    (b) Non-teaching activities

	Aspect	*Observations*	*Action*

3. Career

   (a) Long term view

   (b) College support

Signed: . . . .
                                                        Section Leader

SECTION 4
ISSUES IN
IMPLEMENTING
APPRAISAL

4.1 Formal Teacher Appraisal: Why and How, not If

Ray Sumner

Contexts

We have reached a position where the formal appraisal of teachers will become an accepted practice. For better or worse, non-teaching interests are bidding for greater control over what teachers will teach in schools and colleges. How well they teach has become the subject of legislation. Whether or not being regarded as an outstanding teacher will warrant more pay remains to be seen despite continuing opposition from some teachers' unions (NUT 1983, Garner 1984). Currently, the government is supporting pilot schemes for appraising teachers in six LEAs, following preliminary studies in Suffolk (Suffolk Education Department 1985 and 1987).

Conceptual bases

Whatever emerges, the core concept is judgement of performance. There is a vague hierarchy which runs from

(a)   appraisal of practice; through
(b)   assessment of competence; to
(c)   evaluation of effectiveness.

The lack of clarity as to the nature of the performance evaluation is compounded by the use of various labels, such as 'career review' (Bell 1987), and 'staff development interview' (Monks 1987).
The public debate on the scrutiny of teachers at work encompasses a range of standpoints, such as:
  – social mores (authority v. equality);
  – collective status (professional v. operative);
  – individual morale (self-valuation v. others' valuation);
  – relevance of activities (productiveness v. 'busy-work');
  – locus of control (independence v. subordination);
  – probity of assessors (impartiality v. bias),
  – consistency of judgements – usually called reliability (technical
                                  soundness v. unknown);
  – fidelity (authenticity of teaching model v. mismatch);
  – economic (contributing to growth v. draining the pool).

Several of these distinctions were made in an excellent American review of teacher evaluation (Darling-Hammond et al. 1983). In the paper, the relative positions of evaluator and teacher are juxtaposed in contexts ranging from teaching viewed as a **craft** (where it is rationally planned, programmed, organised and delivered in routine ways) to seeing it as a **profession** (which calls for the craft skills plus a theoretical knowledge necessary to diagnose problems and create solutions). For the craft case, evaluation would entail direct external inspection and judgement against some standard of performance; for the professional case, evaluation would be by peers. Of course, it does not follow that appraisal by a superior shows that the craft view has been adopted; but it might imply that the craft aspects would be judged of most value in performing the job.
Another aspect is that **rationalistic** systems tend to be bureaucratic, in contrast to **naturalistic** systems which accommodate bargaining, lack of consensus, autonomy and decentralised decision-taking. Teachers' individual development might flourish well in the latter setting, whereas the former will seek to promote conformity to organisational goals. The Darling-Hammond review also presents evaluation within the dichotomies of :
(a)   improvement v. accountability; and
(b)   individual v. organisation.

For individual staff development, therefore, the need is for formative information; whereas for personnel management decisions, the information would be summative.

The staff development context seems to imply that either the teachers or the head are not satisfactory, of themselves or to meet a changing situation. In the accountability context either a person or a school is potentially under threat.

Dual role of headteachers

Yet another context stems from the head's situation, in which he or she is held accountable for the effectiveness of teachers in the school. Putting it this way sharply highlights the problem of intrusiveness : of others' values on the one hand; and of one person in another's territory.

Lloyd (1981) reports that heads in primary schools tended to make use of data from outside the classroom. They usually were reluctant to observe performance directly and judged a teacher by taking his or her class when standing in for them. Thus, evidence was obtained from indirect sources, such as pupils' books. Even so, about a quarter of the 50 heads surveyed claimed to have spoken to teachers about perceived deficiencies.

Apart from the low key appraisals, it is probable that heads would prefer to implement an LEA scheme; rather like external examining. Care is needed in this respect because, though teachers might also prefer to have a scheme devised 'by them', it may not provide the type of data which an authority would find most useful. And for some purposes, this information might be the most sensitive legally as well as personally. Undoubtedly, it will be transmitted from the school to remote destinations (files, the computer, pastoral inspector, chief inspector).

Clearly, it is not adequate merely to characterise appraisal purposes as relating to individual staff development or school improvement when it is formative; or to promotion or demotion when it is summative. Typification by organisational ethos and locus assists with clarifying **purposes** within context. For example, when school is the locus, an ethos of control emphasises accountability, target-setting and the prescription of new teaching approaches. In contrast, when the ethos is autonomy, aspects such as job-satisfaction, volunteering for INSET which is personally chosen, and aiming for personal targets become prominent.

The second Suffolk study casts appraisal for headteachers and teachers alike as supporting individual development. The implications of the contexts reviewed previously indicate that the headteacher's review would have the characteristics of autonomy, whilst for teachers the hallmark would be accountability.

The introduction of a scheme can be expected to change the situation with respect to how teachers perceive their own performance and how they believe others will value it. One effect which might be anticipated from the analysis offered above is that even schemes which are seemingly benign are likely to be perceived as threats to autonomy, unless there is no possibility of feedback to an outsider with authority. The implication that formal appraisal impinges heavily on conceptions of professional relationships is quite clear.

Leadership

Positive aspects, such as identifying teachers who might be promoted through encouraging leadership potential, can be presented as enhancing the conduct of professional affairs. The attributes identified with successful leadership are not completely agreed upon (Murgatroyd and Gray 1982) and ideas about their importance can change (Brown et al. 1982). The former writers stress sensitivity and group problem-solving, whilst the latter, from personal construct theory research with principals, showed that perceptiveness and intelligence, self-others orientation, decision-making skills, innovation and leadership qualities (accepts extra responsibilities, organises well, flexible and creative, motivates) ranked most highly, in that order, and that dynamic personality, professional knowledge, teacher rapport and student rapport came low on the list.

Writing of the USA, Murphy et al. (1983) said that research in this field has been subject to major methodological problems, such as generalising from enquiries conducted mainly with elementary school principals; the lack of explanatory models; misconceptions about management and about leadership (dependence on personal qualities like confidence and assertiveness c.f. appropriate response in a given milieu); and, too narrow a focus on the technical aspects of teaching. Leithwood (1982) makes the point that training in managerial skills usually supports a particular preferred style, as derived from research with the managers/leaders; but his view is that attributes associated with notable student growth would be a more appropriate base. However, Blumberg and Greenfield (1980) remark that description is not prescription; they identify five key characteristics not acquired in graduate training, as follows:

(a)   high energy level, willingness to work long hours;

(b)   good expressive abilities;
(c)   proactivity – getting the ball rolling;
(d)   good at listening and observing, at gathering data; and
(e)   skilled in analysing requirements and evaluating alternatives.

The foregoing discussion has brought out the distinction between professional development (doing one's job more effectively, or becoming equipped to do other jobs) and career development. Both contexts require decision-taking. A systematic approach in which the decision-taker is **the central part** of the context is proposed by Chapman (1983). In this framework he places the rewards, requisites and incentives associated with a new job against an individual's values, aptitudes and resources, respectively. He says that in considering career development, it is important to examine the match between a person's values and the rewards of the job (e.g. income with earnings, prestige with respect, independence with autonomy, etc) against the person's resources (pay with funds taken up by training, energy with level of endeavour expected, perseverance with time needed for in-service education).

Techniques

Consideration of appraisal contexts has included the general educational milieu, the specific LEA and school's situation, the purposes and outcomes of appraisal schemes and the personal values and attributes of those assessed. How the appraisals are done will also form part of the context. For the teachers, the extent to which they control the evaluation is likely to mediate its acceptance, as is their confidence in the evaluator (Glasman and Paulin 1982). The available methods include observation, written examinations, activity inventories, interviews, simulations, rating scales and student performance measures, used singly or in combination.

Job analysis

When performance is evaluated (as distinct from, say, leadership potential) there are grounds for basing it on a job analysis, particularly in the USA where the validity of an assessment could be challenged in the courts. A functional job analysis would focus on the work done rather than the qualifications required for access or theoretical background knowledge. It would take in aspects such as task analysis, how much of these tasks a person does and what performance standards are required. Verbs are pre-eminent in describing job functions: e.g. **with data** – computing, analysing, co-ordinating, synthesising; **with people** – serving, persuading, treating, consulting, negotiating; **with things** – handling, manipulating, precision working (Fine 1982).

The blanket application of a single job analysis might be mistaken. In England, Youngman (1983) analysed responses from two samples of teachers to a 245 item self-report questionnaire intended as the basis for a job description instrument. Cluster analyses led to the identification of six intrinsic roles related to some extent to the level of post held by the teacher, length of service, designation and sex. The clusters were described as **administrative, pastoral** and **departmental** and as **practical, involved** and **confined** (i.e. limited to the timetabled classes with little other activity). The main categories of teachers' work were as follows:

(a)   exercise-based teaching;
(b)   resource-based teaching;
(c)   supervision of equipment in use;
(d)   providing pupil work;
(e)   assessing pupils' adjustment;
(f)   pastoral administration;
(g)   school administration;
(h)   constructing a syllabus;
(i)   controlling teaching supplies;
(j)   managing teaching;
(k)   managing staff;
(l)   supervising trainees;
(m)   external liaison;
(n)   examination administration;
(o)   general teaching.

A job analysis using these categories would have different sets of redundant items for teachers occupying each of the six roles identified in the clusters.

Models as a basis

Whereas Youngman's research derived a range of roles associated with teachers' circumstances from teachers' own reports of their activities, other paradigms have been proposed on the premise that effective teaching can be characterised. The second Suffolk report has three major categories,

1.   planning and preparation;

2.   classroom management; and

3.   evaluation.

Each of these is expanded through sets of descriptions; e.g. creates a supportive learning atmosphere by showing concern and respect for every pupil. These resemble aspects of 'the Hunter model' for improving teacher effectiveness, which has 11 components. Four (summarised) examples are :

(a)   deliberate separation of genuine constraints from 'typical ethnic, financial, intellectual or emotional excuses for learning failure';

(b)   identification of productive learning behaviour for each particular pupil;

(c)   investment of self plus competency in the specific learning area to enhance the pupil probability of success; and

(d)   determination to re-teach, reinforce or abandon an approach if an objective is not appropriate for the pupils.

Though the Hunter model is cited approvingly in the Suffolk report, its use in a four-year programme for developing teacher effectiveness was found to be inconsequential by the project evaluators in California (e.g. Stallings et al. (1986), Stallings and Krasavanage (l986), Robbins and Wolfe (1987), and Porter (1986)); and it was severely criticised for its mechanistics and prescriptive features by Gibboney (1987). Despite Hunter's rejoinders (Hunter 1986 and 1987), a cursory analysis of the 11 components shows that it presents a virtually impossible range of requirements for the teacher. One of those instanced above, 'identification of productive learning behaviour for each pupil', as a basis for classroom observation (p.30, second Suffolk report), implies that every lesson and every class will have had this consideration in advance. If this were not the case, a randomly chosen period of observation could miss the occasions when a teacher could demonstrate its accomplishment.

Models tend to present an extremely idealised picture of teaching; but as Broadhead (1987) shows, convincingly, HMI/DES has consistently projected an ideal whilst acknowledging that it represents a goal rather than a practicality. Apart from philosophical issues, *the utility of*

taking an ideal as the standard for judging performance seems highly questionable.
The problem with a highly prescriptive behavioural specification is that the methodology for appraisal is problematic, though at first reading, an operation should be in evidence. The 'verbs' are present in the description defined, so behaviour ought to be measurable (even a checklist is a crude, 0 or 1 measure). We should question, however, whether observers share a common language, are in-tune with the rhetoric, perceive actions in specific contexts in the same way, and utilise the scales in an agreed fashion. It should be noted, however, that Moyles (1987) apparently shows that even aspects such as 'professional attitudes' can be observed and rated on a 0 to 10 scale to the satisfaction of the teachers collaborating in developing a scheme for nursery and infant teachers.

Instrumentation

The foregoing includes instrumentation, the people who use the instruments, procedures for processing and evaluating the data and for feeding back and utilising the information. The possibilities can be set out in a grid, as in Figure 7.

This shows 18 – 22 ways in which information might be gained, assuming that student opinions are admissible. In fact, a mixture of methods, i.e. interview and observation, has been advocated (Second Suffolk Study). An illustration of a different mix comes from Delson-Karan (1982) who was evaluating teaching a foreign language. Observation schedules were developed for : the teacher; the supervisor; and the students.

INSTRUMENT

Assessor	Student Progr.	Exam.	Question-naire	Simul-ation	Observ-ation	Inter-view	Activity Schedule or Diary
Teacher	X	—	X	—	X	—	X
Peer	X	—	?	?	X	?	X
Superior	X	—	—	X	X	X	X
Assessor	X	X	—	X	X	X	—
Student	—	—	X	—	—	—	?

Figure 7 – Possible teaching instruments

The latter had questions about teacher capabilities (enthusiasm, fluency, accent, tone of voice), class participation and rapport with teacher, students' learning, and overall rating of the teacher. A good case can be made for the teacher being his or her own evaluator (Kremer and Ben-Peretz 1984) using criteria of their own choosing and data readily to hand from records or day to day observation, but reliability and comparability would present problems.

In the UK there has been no advocacy for examining teachers, but in the USA a small number of authorities require teachers to take a re-certification examination (Benderson 1982). Also, observational procedures of a somewhat stringent kind are used in some districts which have trained observers or teams of three observers, these noting pre-set lesson features (Blackmer et al. 1981). Research into the fidelity of schedules has been carried out partly in relation to the quality of information yielded by *high inference* and *low inference* schedules (Murray 1983; Wiersma et al. 1983). The distinction concerns attributes such as 'student involvement', which has to be inferred by an observer, in contrast to specific behaviours, such as 'provided for group discussion', which require no inference. This distinction might be associated with teaching which is didactic or focused on low level skills. This is quite distinct from less directive teaching aimed at problem-solving and subtle understandings. *One conclusion of note is that behavioural attributes appear differently when different instruments are used; in other words, there is instrument variation*.

The two most widely used techniques are rating scales and interviews, with the latter being currently favoured in this country. However, some emerging schemes employ qualitative ratings (i.e. satisfactory, good, very good) to a range of defined responsibilities, and their use for self-appraisal, by a peer and by a visiting assessor, might be investigated. Basically, this approach aims to derive a standard set of activities and provide a common structure for appraisal. There is no attempt to reach agreement on the meaning of the rating points. To be regarded as reliable, this kind of instrument should be investigated for inter-rater consistency within rater type and between types of raters. More technically developed sets of instruments are known as *behaviourally anchored rating scales* (BARS); also *behavioural observation scales* (BOS). Duignan (1982), for example, had one group of principals identify aspects of their own behaviour when they had been effective; another group then assigned the separate behaviours to cognate groups; finally, a third group wrote descriptions of extreme performances both 'good' and 'poor', and of intermediate performances which were given numerical values on the 1 – 5 scale.

Descriptor ambiguities and inconsistencies in assigning numerical values were eliminated during the process. The scales were concerned with problem-solving, decision-making, communicating with staff, delegating to others, introducing innovation, educational leadership, managing conflict, managing time, managing stress, relating to others, supervising staff, and allocating resources. It should be noted that the scales are not concerned with global activity, but with certain key activities bearing on effective performance in a role. The examples of a BARS given in the second Suffolk report (p.85) is a travesty; it includes impossible behaviour ('talks with God', 'walks on water'). The excerpt from the HMI lesson observation schedule (p.86) shows a high inference level in certain respects (e.g. 'pupils' capabilities not extended at all'), which is acceptable when a consensus is believed to exist; otherwise, the reliable application of descriptions would need to be developed and evaluated in trials.

Another technically complex development procedure is used to construct a *performance appraisal system* (PAS) (Sokol 1982). The steps are :

1. identify a group of superior performers (from supervisors lists, peer nominations and records);

2. identify a control group of average performers;

3. construct a 'competency model' (by focusing on such 'critical events' as those which test effectiveness);

4. ascertain what qualities an incumbent would look for if finding someone to do their job; and

5. retain only aspects of competence which differentiate the two criterion groups.

Assessors are then trained in using the PAS, organised into an interview or expressed as behavioural rating scales.

Feedback

Clearly, interviews which probe and elicit involve personal interaction and this depends to some extent on the differences between the superior and the subordinate being minimised. Another kind of ethos has been established for procedures designed to help teachers who acknowledge that they are experiencing undue difficulties in their classrooms (Montgomery 1984). Teacher evaluation is carried out by an observer who writes notes throughout a lesson so as to provide the basis for verifiable feedback to the teacher and discussion of various events. The teacher's behaviour is analysed by reference to a tactical lesson plan which has three main facets drawn from theory. These are *catch them being good* (CBG), to enable behaviour modification; *positive cognitive intervention* (PCI), to build up pupils' involvement in learning; and *management, monitoring and maintenance phases* (3M's).

At first a regular lesson is observed but later on, lessons planned using the principles embodied in the model are observed. It is evident that observers need training in how to behave in the classroom and handle feedback supportively, concentrating on implications from the model rather than prescribing 'how to do it'. In this sense they act as consultants but interact as peers with the teacher concerned.

Multi-techniques

Some of the methods described above are obviously practical and relevant and can be organised fairly conveniently. For other aspects of the jobs done by teachers, there may be a case for conducting appraisals via simulated tasks drawing on sample of the work dealt with from time to time. Also, a period of training for a new activity which is an essential part of a promotion post or new job could be used for assessing future performance, a concept integral to 'trainability testing' (Seigel 1982). Combining these techniques with interviews or observation would certainly add richness and credibility to a procedure.

Conclusion

Some of the techniques described would suit schools rather than constitute elements of LEA-wide procedures. It would be regrettable, however, if the advent of an LEA appraisal scheme cut across methods individual schools may have evolved which are linked to staff development. And it remains to be seen whether the context of accountability for the quality of teaching in a school can be compatible with a programme of staff development. Perhaps this will best be served by the use of two or more complementary techniques or types of appraiser, including teachers' peers. It is to be hoped that the subtleties of the contexts discussed earlier will be recognised and that several of the techniques described will be trialled and evaluated within contexts before conclusions are reached about the efficacy, acceptability, and logistical feasibility of any particular scheme.

4.2 Management Issues in the Introduction of an Appraisal Scheme

Bob Cooper and John West-Burnham

Introduction

The introduction of any new system into an organisation poses problems for the manager. With something as sensitive as the introduction of an appraisal scheme into a school or college at this particular moment in time, the problems are especially acute. Good management is undoubtedly required, firstly, if the proposed scheme is to be accepted by the staff as a whole and, secondly, if the new procedures are to lead to greater effectiveness in relation to the essential purposes of the school which are to facilitate the education of children. In any process of change the way in which that change is managed is as important as the fact of change itself. If the change is to be absorbed into the culture of the organisation and is to become an accepted and integral part of day-to-day working practices, it is crucial both to consider and to follow sound management principles in relation to the problems which inevitably will be encountered.

One way of categorising the problems involved is to consider them from two ends of a continuum, *firstly, looking at them from a whole school or systems end, and, secondly, looking at the problems in relation to the individuals concerned*. In the first case, that is from the macro point of view, one would consider such things as the structures, the organisation and the control mechanisms; and in the second, or micro case, one would need to look at the individuals, how they are going to perceive the changes, what interpersonal skills will be needed in handling the situation, what responses are likely from that individual, etc. Of course it is recognised that in the reality of a school or college this kind of dichotomy is a false one. You cannot in practice separate the bureaucratic procedures you wish to introduce, from the context in which they are to operate and the people who will be affected by them. Management is a complex inter-related activity which needs to take account of all aspects of a situation and to balance judgements about one part of an equation with decisions about the risks involved elsewhere. With that disclaimer in mind, it is here proposed to consider a number of key issues which all managers will have to face when they are contemplating the introduction of an appraisal scheme into their institution. The relative importance of these aspects will vary according to the individual school or college, and there is no attempt here to prioritise these various factors.

Managing the change

The implementation of any form of change into a school or college requires careful planning. There is much research evidence available to show that careful planning of the implementation of a change initiative can be crucial to the ultimate success of the enterprise. This does not mean, of course, that the plan itself should be absolute and inflexible. It needs to be capable of adaptation, as well as being able to take account of the views of others. When thinking about the introduction of an appraisal scheme it is necessary to think about both content and process. The content in this case includes such matters as documentation, who will have access to the documentation, the form and nature of the interview, the time needed and how it will be found, etc. The process will include a consideration of what meetings need to take place, how the ideas might best be discussed, when is the most appropriate time to start the discussions, how much time should be left before decisions are taken, etc. (See final suggested action plan, 5.1). For effective change to take place it is necessary to understand the nature of the change process. Whatever strategies are used to initiate change there is a need to ensure that the mechanisms introduced fit into the established culture of the organisation. Whatever procedures are decided upon they should fit into the established culture of the organisation. They should not be simply bolted onto the existing structures but should grow as a logical extension out of existing good practice. If you try to transplant something too alien into a living body it will be rejected. Going through the motions of change is not enough. There needs to be a real acceptance of the change on the part of staff who have to operate it.

Staff are more likely to accept change if it is perceived by them as something which is both beneficial and relevant in some way to their jobs. If they can be encouraged to at least try the process they may then discover that sitting down with a colleague for an hour talking about themselves, receiving feedback and recognition of their efforts, and having the opportunity to discuss future aims in a constructive atmosphere does have some merit.

The introduction of any change into an organisation has resource implications and these need to be fully taken into account. In the case of appraisal it is necessary to calculate not only the possible financial costs of initial training and follow-up support, but also the time involved in the process of change and over subsequent years. If change is to be effected these opportunity costs should be recognised and fully audited.

As Fullan (1985) has pointed out all change involves learning, and we are here talking about learning which is very different from children's learning. There are both formal and informal aspects to be taken into account, and there is an important emotional element to consider.

Leadership style

One of the problems when we are talking about educational organisations is that they are never simple closed systems. Schools and colleges have been referred to as organised anarchies because their goals are generally ill-defined, complex and frequently contradictory and also because the various sub-units within the institution are often pursuing goals that are unrelated to the broader general and explicit aims of the organisation as a whole. Whatever the purpose of introducing an appraisal scheme into the institution might be, and it can be seen from the case studies reported in this book and from a variety of other accounts (Trethowan 1987, Strike and Millman 1983), these purposes can vary considerably, one effect which can be anticipated is that even schemes which are designed and advertised as non-threatening are likely to be perceived as a threat to individual autonomy by some teachers and lecturers. This needs to be clearly recognised whether the scheme which is being introduced is one which has been developed internally or whether it is one which is being imposed on the institution by the local authority.

All organisations have a unique and distinctive ethos or climate just as all managers have a management style which affects that ethos. Climate in an organisation is not like the rain in Manchester which has to be accepted with a good grace. It is something which is a result of individual human interaction. Whatever the general overall leadership style might be and whatever the overall management strategies adopted by the chief manager in a school or college, it would be advisable to adopt in this case an organic style which could accommodate bargaining, negotiation and participation in the decision-making process, rather than attempting to impose a change. Staff need time to adjust to change and if they have been involved in the processes leading up to the change they are more likely to accept it. This sounds elementary but it is surprising in practice how often it is not carried through. We still have in many cases the image of the head or the principal as the captain of the ship, whose job it is to make the decisions and to issue orders which must be obeyed unquestioningly by the crew. There is an increasing amount of evidence now both from research and from studies of good management practice that the most successful educational institutions like the most successful firms in industry and business, are those in which the staff of that organisation feel that their views are fully taken into account. This does not necessarily mean that you have the kind of democratic system in which the view of the majority is always taken. On the whole, staff recognise that the principal or the head has responsibilities and that because of these responsibilities he or she has at times to take decisions which are contrary to the view of a majority, perhaps because of external constraints. If, however, there has been a real discussion of the issues involved, and staff feel that it has been recognised that they have a point of view and their opinions have been canvassed they are more likely to accept and work within changed circumstances.

A participative style of decision-making does take time. One of the problems in schools and colleges is that there is very little acknowledgement of the need to find time for management purposes. The training of a teacher does not take account of the fact that one day the teacher may be promoted and may have management responsibilities which are certainly equivalent to those of the managing director of a small firm. There is a tendency for teachers and lecturers to feel that unless they are in a classroom teaching a group of students they are not really working, and that time spent upon meetings is somehow extraneous. In some cases of course it is because the meetings which are called are not to seek opinion but simply to tell the staff what has been decided. This, if anything, makes matters worse because staff recognise it as a pseudo decision-making process, and they also resent their time being wasted.

Middle management

The idea of the appraisal interview comes from industrial management practice where it has been used by many industries and firms for a number of years. It is used both for an evaluative purpose in order to consolidate judgments about the effectiveness of individual job performance and also for identifying career and development needs. It is generally part of accepted management practice in industry and is an integral part of the way in which individual managers think about their role and the responsibilities it entails. As a manager you accept to a greater or lesser extent the responsibility for the efficient working of your section of the firm, and you also accept that it entails responsibility for evaluating the effective working of your subordinates. You also accept that you have a responsibility to those above you for the way in which you do your job.

Almost all schools seek to implement their policies by creating structures which reflect varying levels of status, authority, responsibility and accountability. This is normally a reflection of the promoted posts available combined with the perspective of the headteacher as to the most effective way to implement policy and ensure effective administrations at appropriate levels. The structures which are created in schools will usually try to reflect the need to communicate and delegate effectively, to facilitate planning, decision-making and evaluation and to enable leadership and motivation. It is in this latter category that appraisal is a highly significant management strategy. Equally the outcomes of the appraisal process may well facilitate the other components of management.

One of the facts of life for the chief manager in a school or college is that all the members of the teaching staff are professional people, and many of them feel that as such they should have a great deal of individual autonomy in relation to the work they do with students in the classroom. Many teachers indeed feel that their only accountability, and therefore their only real responsibility in the job is to the children and they therefore have every right to keep the classroom door shut. Strangely enough this demand for autonomy often does not extend to the way in which decisions are made about the organisation as a whole. Often teachers and lecturers are quite prepared to abrogate all their responsibilities for this to the head or the management team.

In a small organisation such as a primary school it is possible for the headteacher to undertake the appraisal of all the staff in the school. In a larger school or college this would not generally be practicable over a substantial period of time. Some heads or principals might decide to do the first batch of interviews themselves in order to launch the scheme and to signal the importance they attach to the process. However if it were to be done in this way on the first occasion it is questionable whether the head of a large institution should spend the amount of time necessary to do the job properly in this way every year. It is generally better in a larger institution to delegate the responsibility for conducting the interviews down the line. The delegated responsibility is usually appreciated by those who receive it and will in many cases be a real staff development activity for them.

It has been found through working with heads of department in secondary schools and with section leaders in further and higher education that *at this middle management level there is often little recognition of any real management responsibility for the members of staff below them in their departments*. When asked about their role they have described it as that of a glorified post boy, whose job it is to pass on the decisions of the senior management team to their colleagues and to pass upwards requests for materials or in-service training from their departmental staff to the appropriate deputy. Middle managers in a large school need to feel that they have a real responsibility for the efficient working of the department as a whole and for the staff development of its individual members. Undertaking the appraisal interview can often lead to a much clearer definition of the middle managers' role both within the organisation generally and on the part of individual heads of department.

The subject or pastoral team forms the natural focus for the management of staff as well as the implementation of the curriculum and pastoral care. It permits a level of specialist knowledge and skill to be developed, the team leader has an appropriate 'span of control', he or she is able to know the team personally, there is a commonality of expertise and interest and frequent contact.

Staff development needs are thus best identified and delivered at the appropriate functional level, be it the infants department of three teachers or the science faculty of 12 teachers. Locating the responsibility for appraisal at the level of head of department helps to link authority and responsibility at the appropriate level. It equally creates the appropriate structure for the appraisal of middle managers by creating reciprocal responsibility between middle and senior management. Such relationships require explicit analysis, negotiation and descriptions if they are to function effectively. This involves the use of job descriptions which need to be differentiated from conditions of employment, which are generic and job lists which are descriptive. Job descriptions are derived from a process of job analysis, are individually negotiated and subject to renegotiation and form the basis of the appraisal process.

The appraisal interview can thus serve to clarify the role of the middle manager and enhance relationships within the team.

Staff development

The relationship between appraisal and staff development is symbiotic. Appraisal lacks validity unless it is within the context of development and it is difficult to envisage how staff development can be managed without some form of appraisal.

The management of staff development requires the co-ordination of a number of elements; the teacher's perception of his or her own needs; the stated objectives of the school and the activities necessary to achieve them; the means of diagnosing those needs and the mechanisms for implementation and evaluation. Equally staff development can only function effectively if it is a component of a process of whole school improvement which combines institutional needs with the requirements of central government, LEA and community. In the final analysis the function of staff development is to enhance the experiences of children in the classroom.

Given the complexity of this range of demands a systematic approach to staff development is imperative. Such a system involves:

1. A statement of school aims which are translated into objectives, i.e. specific actions leading to defined outcomes within a clear timescale. Without such a statement, staff development will inevitably lack focus and priorities.

2. A process of needs assessment. For the school this might involve the use of GRIDS or DION or any process of whole school review. For the individual teacher the relevant process is appraisal as a means of relating individual expectations and requirements to departmental and school requirements.

3. Reconciling the discrepancies between what the school aspires to do and its current situation. The shortfall between where the school wants to be, its objectives, and where it is, based on institutional and individual review, represents the agenda for staff development.

4. Having diagnosed needs it is then necessary to establish which resources are available to the school through a process of resource audit. The individual appraisal interview is the basis for this, identifying strengths as well as needs and recognising that staff development is proactive as well as reactive.

5. Instituting a staff development programme in which the needs of staff are reconciled with the available skills and knowledge within the school, the demand for external provision is assessed and a programme instituted on the basis of prioritisation of resources available.

6. The final stage in the staff development model – evaluation and appraisal – constitutes a significant element of this process facilitating, as it does, a review of individual activities against known objectives.

This system presupposes a school ethos geared to institutional improvement, the acceptance of staff development as both an individual responsibility and a central management function and the skills of diagnosis, analysis and prioritising.

Motivation

In the context of whole school improvement through staff development emerging from parallel processes of institutional review and individual appraisal, the motivation of teachers is crucial. Most theories of leadership see motivation as one of the key functions and responsibilities of the leader.

In the educational context this view is potentially problematic, given the varying perceptions as to what constitutes a 'leader', the claim to individual professional autonomy, and the notion that teaching is a self-legitimating activity, in which the rewards are implicit to the activity and so praise and recognition of teachers are unnecessary. Against this have to be set the facts that teachers are employees working in hierarchical relationships within organisations. Equally the achievement of objectives and the creation of a culture of growth, improvement and enhancement requires individuals to operate over and above prescribed norms, if a purely functional bureaucratic approach is to be avoided and involvement and creativity valued.

Individuals at work will be guided in their behaviour by their perceptions of the interaction of three factors: the expectation that a certain level of effort will lead to desired performance; the linking of that performance to a desired outcome, and the value placed upon the outcomes.

The nature of the outcomes will vary between teachers and will vary across time for each individual. Whatever is perceived as being a potentially valuable outcome will therefore have significance as a motivating factor. Such outcomes may either be defined in terms of the individual's psychological needs, e.g. achievement, recognition, a sense of being valued, or may be external factors such as salary, working conditions, management policy and processes within the school. There cannot be a hierarchy of such outcomes given that they are particular to the individual and only have significance in a given context at a particular time.

The appraisal process has a significant role to play in facilitating the motivation of individual teachers. The interview provides a significant opportunity for various forms of recognition and for facilitating the other factors. Equally through the link with staff development strategies it is possible to facilitate activities that the teacher believes to be of personal value which also have implications for school improvement.

A properly managed appraisal process provides the opportunity for enhancing communication and thereby developing and improving interpersonal relationships within the organisational structure of the school. Of itself, this process can be seen as one of valuing the individual whilst enhancing their contribution to the school.

Training

Whilst appraisal is a key component in the diagnosis of training needs, it represents a key development activity in itself. Indeed, in contemplating establishing an appraisal system consideration should be given to appropriate training and development relevant to the process itself.

Three broad areas for development may be identified: the process of staff development; appraisal skills; and developing perspectives on change.

The skills and knowledge relevant to the **management of staff development** are wide-ranging and complex but the following might be identified as crucial:
–the diagnosis of needs;
–the establishing of priorities;
–the design of activities;
–the delivery of activities;
–knowledge of teachers' learning patterns;
–knowledge of resources inside the school;
–knowledge of provision available outside the school.

Appraisal skills are complex, involving, as they do, interpersonal factors: the following are particularly relevant in this context:
–listening and questioning skills;
–knowledge of factors influencing attitudes in the interview;
–negotiating skills;
–knowledge of motivation.

Managing change involves a broader range of skills and knowledge:
–knowledge of the school as a social entity;

–awareness of micropolitics;
–knowledge of management techniques;
–understanding the process of change;
–knowledge and skills in evaluation.

All of these elements are implicit to the successful introduction and management of a staff development strategy based on appraisal. It is important, however, to see these elements as part of a dynamic process which enhances knowledge and skills on the one hand and applies and evaluates them on the other. If appraisal is to be a formative process, then the school mechanisms of appraisal must be capable of development and improvement, and not be seen as a bureaucratic procedure which is simply concerned with generating a list of staff development activities. *The enhancement of personal relationships is an equally significant outcome.*

Interpersonal skills

All management involves working with and through people. The introduction of an appraisal scheme requires the exercise of all the interpersonal skills which are a necessary part of all management and in particular require a consideration of the skills needed for the interview itself. Some of these are considered in greater depth in Section 4.3.

The appraisal interview is a social situation requiring social skills and, like all social situations, the venue needs to be considered carefully. If the person conducting the interview has an office, then that can be used. In many cases, however, in schools and colleges the person conducting the interview may not have a separate private room of their own. It is important that the interview should be conducted in a place without interruption from people or telephones. If the whole is to be a success, there is a need for both parties to be able to concentrate on the matter in hand without distraction.

A range of social skills is needed in the course of the interview itself. In general there are seven major steps in the process and at each stage a variety of interactive skills is required.

1.   Step one is a preparation stage when the appraisee needs to be contacted and a time and place decided upon. The way in which this is done needs to be considered so that the tone of the exercise is set. If the appraisee perceives that they are being

summoned to appear it may be difficult to help them to relax. If, however, things are too casual, there is a danger that the whole thing will not be given importance and then vital preparation will be neglected. As in almost all social situations, a balance needs to be struck.

2.   The second step is concerned with the opening of the interview when it is important to establish a relaxed and friendly tone. It is usually advisable at this stage to restate the purpose of the interview and to define the roles being taken.

3.   The third step is to discuss the appraisee's self-assessment of their work over the preceding period. The important skill involved here is active listening. Some teachers and lecturers find this particularly difficult (see Section 4.3).

4.   The fourth step is to share data about how the appraisee's performance in the job is seen by the appraiser. This feedback, which will include both positive recognition and constructive comments on achievements, is at the heart of the whole process. It is a process of helping the member of staff for whom the appraiser has a management responsibility to face the efficiency and effectiveness with which they are performing their job.

5.   Step five is to summarise the results of the joint analysis. If there are areas of disagreement about some aspects of the job, they need to be faced. However, the appraisal interview is not a disciplinary interview. If such an interview is needed then it should take an entirely different form and requires different social skills. The purpose of the appraisal interview is essentially review and development and the whole should be conducted in that light.

6.   The sixth step is to develop an action plan or to discuss future targets. This may involve tempering enthusiasm in some cases or encouraging the taking of responsibility in others.

7.   Finally, the interview needs to be closed with a further summary and reinforcement of praise to end on a positive note.

The interview does not take place in a vacuum and there are ongoing relationships to consider. In some cases there is a personal and social friendship which extends outside the workplace and into the home. This should not inhibit either the conduct or the rigour with which the interview is conducted. In other cases the appraiser may genuinely feel at the end of the interview that there is so much personal antipathy or antagonism between them as part of an ongoing work relationship that the appraisal process has not been successful. In this case the problem should be addressed, perhaps by bringing the issue to the attention of the appraiser's superior and seeing if, by bringing the issues into the open, a more satisfactory working relationship can be achieved.

Conclusion

To talk of managing appraisal creates an artificial impression of its status. Appraisal has to be seen as a crucial component of effective school management and not a discrete activity. If the appraisal process becomes a bureaucratic ritual, then it not only fails in its essential purpose but may actually become counter-productive. Appraisal is thus a constituent of an overall strategy which enables staff development to take place and enhance school effectiveness.

However, given the political context and the inconsistent environment in which appraisal is being introduced, its introduction has to be managed in such a way that it becomes integral to the working of a school and teachers insist on their right to be appraised.

4.3 Conducting Effective Appraisal Interviews

Keith Diffey

Introduction

There is no one best way to conduct an appraisal interview. If there were, the whole activity would be a manipulative operation rather than a complex human skill. Furthermore, the assumption that anyone can sit down for a chat about a teacher's job, avoid the pitfalls and make it a purposeful and worthwhile event, is naive. There are skills involved which need learning and developing. Many staff in schools are very experienced in the skills of interviewing – with pupils, parents and potential employees. However, the wholesale application of generic interviewing techniques to the unique encounter of an appraisal interview is inappropriate:

> The appraisal interview is not like any other interview the manager is likely to have to conduct. It is private, usually, and the parties may be bound in confidence not to reveal what went on. It does not – should not – have the flavour of evaluation which selection interviews, and dismissal interviews, often have.
>
> Stewart & Stewart (1977)

Effective appraisal interviewing does not only depend upon the conduct of the participants 'during' the actual encounter. It also depends upon what goes on 'before' the interview, and what takes place 'after' it is over. In this I will offer some guidance on these three stages although in the context of interviewing most of my comments will be concerned with the interactive skills needed whilst the interview is taking place.

> The key to successful appraisal is the interview itself, which should aim to achieve an agreed course of action, and, more significantly, a commitment to a change in behaviour.
>
> Suffolk Education Department (1987)

Before the interview

An effective appraisal interview is more likely to take place in an existing climate of mutual trust and respect. The appraiser must cultivate this atmosphere throughout the whole year – *it can not be conjured up for one occasion.*

> The appraisal interview is not something that is simply plugged in at a certain time. To be effective, the appraisal interview must be viewed as a continuation of professional and personal relationships between the teacher and evaluator.
>
> Haefele (1981)

The appraiser must review all records and previous history and gather all the facts about past performance and future developments. Both participants must understand how the system operates and have faith in it.

Clearly the appraiser must have considerable knowledge about the job that is done by the appraisee. The use of job descriptions and classroom observation is essential, not least because they assist in the negotiation of agreed performance criteria. One legitimate cause of complaint from appraisees is that appraisers simply do not know enough about the work they do, either because they have not taken the trouble to find out, or, because they have not done the job themselves.

Care must be taken to get the environment for the interview right – a private place, office perhaps, without interruptions or telephone calls and plenty of time to complete the interview. Finally the interview must be carefully planned. Proformas should be completed well in advance and the appraisee given notice of the meeting. *Most important, thought must be given to what you want to achieve and how you are going to achieve it.*

During the interview

It is obviously important to pay attention to both content and process. I suggest that content should be largely determined by the appraisee within a broad framework that might include a 'look back' and a 'look

ahead'. Problem areas should be identified by the job holder himself –
in self-appraisal schemes, appraisees are often very critical of themselves. The appraisee should be given time to detail, at his own pace,
his achievements during the year and his future aims and objectives.
It should also give him time to update his career aspirations, seek aid in
following these through and examine how obstacles to progress can best
be overcome.

Cave and Cave (1985)

Techniques of appraisal interviewing

Knowledge is slowly accumulating on the relationships between interviewer behaviour and the subsequent responses of the interviewee.
An awareness of these developments is an essential prerequisite if
appraisers are to develop the necessary skills to conduct appraisal
interviews.

(i)   *The structure of an appraisal interview*

Randell et al. (1984) have suggested that the appraisal interview has
three main stages:
  (a)   an opening – where observations are checked, data is
          gathered and comparisons made;
  (b)   a middle – where an attempt is made to achieve a
          development step;
  (c)   a summing up – where conclusions are agreed and the
          next step is planned.

Fletcher (1973) has identified a sequential 13-stage guide on which to
structure the interview. However, following a rigid structure in a
teacher appraisal interview would create difficulties where the emphasis is on self-appraisal.
Obviously at the beginning of the interview it is necessary to put the
appraisee at ease and establish rapport. Whilst informality is important, *it should always be borne in mind that the appraisal interview
is a professional occasion and needs to be treated as such*. So far as
the appraisee is concerned, lack of appreciation of the importance of
showing that one has a sense of occasion can devalue the event. An air
of enforced joviality and false good humour on the appraiser's part
may increase rather than decrease apprehension.

The appraiser must adapt his ways of controlling discussion to the situation or phase of the interview. The chief variations in control are to be found in:

    (a)   the relative amount of talking done by each participant;
    (b)   the tempo of the interview;
    (c)   the degree of freedom allowed to the appraisee;
    (d)   the degree to which digressions are allowed;
    (e)   the emotional tension or relaxation.

In an appraisal interview I would suggest that the interviewer should control the interview with a loose rein. The most effective influence on attitudes and opinions will come from the appraisee stating the problem in his own words and perhaps by allowing him to overstate his case and thus see the weaknesses for himself, rather than from trying to ram views home. This is especially important when the emphasis is on self-appraisal.

(ii)   *Behaviour shaping approaches*

An awareness of the transactional nature of dyadic communication is fundamental to effective appraisal interviewing. Alteration of one person's behaviour produces changes in the other; therefore the best way to begin improving one's performance in an interview is to undergo personal improvements. These changes relate specifically to one's own behaviour in order that interactive skills may be developed. Interactive skills are the skills used in face-to-face encounters to arrange our behaviour so that it is in step with our objectives. In so far as the other person's judgements about us stem from their observations of our behaviour it is clear that behaviour matters very much. Amongst several other factors, the behaviour of participants, notably that of the appraiser, is one of the crucial items that helps to determine success in the interview. The following hypothetical encounter in an appraisal interview illustrates my thesis.

An appraiser makes the following comment to an appraisee:

> Ben, you've had a difficult year. I must admit that there are several other teachers in the faculty who, like you, have found it difficult to teach the less able.

Some empathy for Ben's situation is expressed but the implication of the statement is that the perceived problem is Ben's and not a school problem. Ben may react negatively:

> I feel I have been treated unfairly! I have four classes of less able kids and I have to pack up and move rooms four times a day! By the time I reach the

classroom, the pupils are running around and throwing chalk. It takes 15 minutes to calm them down. Nobody has offered any assistance – I don't think the problem is all my fault.

The appraiser has misinterpreted previous information and he should be prepared to modify his perception in the light of this new information and use it in a constructive way:

In other words, Ben, you feel that you've been placed in a very difficult teaching situation. I can understand your reaction. You've mentioned a major factor I seem to have overlooked.

Thus the appraiser is prepared to change his original judgement. Ben is more likely to view this kind of interview as worthwhile and feel that the appraiser is concerned about the problem and wishes to help. Ben can now begin to react constructively to the problem. Because an important objective of the appraisal interview is to determine what can be done to improve teaching performance, the appraiser might offer assistance through a statement such as:

Ben, you have been unintentionally placed in a difficult teaching situation. However what do you think we can do to help you with this problem?

The appraiser not only accepts substantial responsibility for Ben's unsatisfactory performance but also indicates that a co-operatively developed plan might alleviate this problem. For example, the appraiser agrees to meet two of Ben's classes as they enter the classroom and a more experienced teacher volunteers to cover the other two groups until Ben arrives. Ben is committed to this plan because he had a personal stake in its creation. The key to a satisfactory outcome is the *change in the behaviour of the appraiser*.

This example illustrates also that an appraisal interview is a two-way process. Appraisers should be sensitive to the fact that they can learn a lot about their own performance during the interview although this should not be allowed to intrude upon the appraisee's self-orientation. Appraisal by subordinates is a legitimate activity and can be undertaken by the use of a questionnaire, for example (Diffey 1986).

There is a vital bond between objectives and behaviour. *One of the indicators of an interactively skilled person is that they frequently declare their objectives, openly and explicitly*. Behaviour needs to be in step with objectives and should be consciously organised and controlled to achieve this. Behaviour shaping is a 'natural' process anyway – by making it a conscious one we harness the behaviour shaping processes more efficiently. If we could only shape behaviour more effectively, cynical comments such as, 'When all is said and done, far more is said than done', need never apply to an appraisal interview.

(iii)   *The use of questions*

The chief tool of the interviewer is the question. The purposes of an appraisal interview will not be served if the questions imply criticism or disagreement by the appraiser. 'Closed' or 'limiting' questions are capable of being answered 'yes' or 'no' or very briefly, with little scope for the appraisee to influence the answer he gives. Questions can be rephrased in terms of degree, for example: 'How happy are you with your job?', rather than, 'Are you happy with your job?' The use of 'leading' and 'multiple' questions is not recommended. 'Do you not think that ...' may be a verbal mannerism but it is also a leading question.

The appraisal interview uses three primary sets of verbal questions: **probing, understanding** (reflective), and **supporting.** Typically, interviewers begin probing questions with 'general leads'. Depending on the response, there may be a 'follow-up lead'. 'Continuation leads' are questions designed to get the appraisee to continue talking about a particular point he is explaining whereas 'amplification leads' are used when the appraiser wants the appraisee to give him more information by further explanation. Often the appraisee transmits signals that there are particular things he would like to talk about. These cues need to be picked up and explored if they are relevant to the objectives of the interview. The pacing and direction of the interview should be largely responsive to the cues – verbal and non-verbal – that the interviewee is giving out. It is a mistake to switch topics too abruptly; bridging comments about where one is going are needed.

The technique of **reflection** is crucial to appraisal interviewing because it lends itself to developing conditions of empathy and acceptance. It is critical for the appraisee to perceive the appraiser as a person who is capable of understanding him on his terms, and the frequent and liberal use of these understanding techniques can be highly effective in generating this perception. The use of these questions conveys that the appraiser is listening 'actively', not passively. The characteristics of reflective responses as outlined by Weber (1978) include:

1.   Greater emphasis on listening rather than talking.

2.   Responding to what is personal rather than abstract.

3.   Following the other in his exploration rather than leading him into areas we think he should be exploring.

4.   Clarifying what the appraisee has said rather than telling him. This is achieved by the use of restatement and paraphrase.

5.   Responding to the 'feelings' implicit in what the other has said rather than the assumptions or content that he has talked about. The appraiser should respond not only to the words that are being expressed, but also to the 'music' that he hears.

6.   Trying to get into the other person's frame of reference rather than listening or responding from our own frame of reference.

7.   Responding with empathic understanding rather than with disconcern or distanced objectivity.

The third category of verbal behaviours – **supporting** – is arguably the most important. If the appraiser can 'share' an experience, point of view, or attitude, very briefly, sometimes this is seen by the appraisee as very supportive. 'Consoling', or sharing one's feelings of concern for the other person, can be effective when the appraisee is threatened by facing himself and his relations with others. Appraisal interviewing is not a mechanical, impersonal activity, and sometimes it is necessary for the appraiser to express whatever 'caring' he feels about the appraisee and his situation which is being explored in the interview. One can not overestimate the importance of maintaining a positive emotional atmosphere because the data gathered via an appraisal interview can be no better than the perceptions of the relationship formed by the two participants.

(iv)   *Further techniques*

Jessup and Jessup (1975) have outlined a range of other techniques validated by research evidence which helps the interviewer achieve certain objectives.
For example the appraisee will talk more if:
    (a)   he or she is looked in the eye and smiled at as you ask a question or as you reach the end of what you have to say;
    (b)   he or she is not interrupted;
    (c)   open-ended questions are asked;
    (d)   an active attitude is adopted.

The appraisee will stop talking or change topic if you:
    (a)   look away from him;
    (b)   sit forward or move your arms forward.

The use of 'confirming responses' is a valuable technique in that it fulfils the other's needs, thus opening him up so that he can fully respond to you. Confirming responses are those that acknowledge the other, clarify what he said, give a supportive response, agree about content, and express positive feelings. Conversely, a disconfirming response is one that is irrelevant, tangential, impersonal, incoherent or incongruent. Understanding the relationship you are in, knowing what function you wish it to serve, and being aware that the rules for it are set forth by you and the other participant are the first steps towards interactive competence.

Overt disagreement tends to generate an aggressive reaction:

> Negative feedback not only fails to motivate, but can cause him to perform worse. Only those employees who have a high degree of self-esteem appear to be stimulated by criticism to improve performance.
>
> Lusty (1981)

One can avoid being tempted into the **disagreement spiral** by pretending that a difficulty has been stated when the other disagrees – this is much more likely to lead to a constructive response. Instead of disagreeing yourself, outline a difficulty and try to build upon this.

It is important also for participants to be aware of their moods, biases, and the 'halo effect'. Your emotional state or mood may have a profound effect on your ability to perceive the other's responses. Biases and prejudices are learned from our culture and may influence perception. Being impressed with or disliking one particular attribute of a person may influence our judgment about other attributes or facts about him – thus the 'halo effect'. In an appraisal interview we make judgements on the basis of the information available based on our own knowledge and beliefs about human nature.

(v)   *Difficult people and topics*

At a meeting of appraisers in Altwood school in July 1984 three types of interviewees were identified:

1.   Keen – often new staff.

2.   Accepting – often middle ranking staff and/or established in post.

3.   Going through the motions – some older established, stable staff.

The last category presents the most difficulty in appraisal interviewing. Appraisees may be over talkative, impatient, dogmatic, destructive, unco-operative, or inattentive.

In dealing with such people the appraiser needs a very high level of interpersonal skill and should, when possible, de-personalize the issue, often by the use of questions which refer the appraisee back to the main objective:

Do you feel we are making progress ...?
Shall we agree to leave that point for the time being?
How does this point of view help us to reach a solution?

Among difficult topics are issues involving criticism of other members of staff, and criticisms of school policy.

In extreme cases, there may be a need to raise a serious teaching problem that has not been disclosed by the appraisee. A developmental self-appraisal interview is not the occasion to do this in my view. A separate interview should be arranged to deal with the specific problem.

People who are over-anxious tend often to withdraw from communication or communicate defensively. Appraisers can help relieve their anxiety by showing patience, trust and honesty. Tolerate silences and digressions; do not appear clinically neutral but establish personal sympathies and affinities.

In a genuine two-way exchange, both participants should leave the interview feeling that they have benefited from the encounter. Stewart and Stewart (1977) succinctly describe the ideal outcome from both points of view:

If the interview was skillfully conducted, he will feel at the end of it that he has a greater insight into the job he has to do; a better idea of where it fits in the rest of the company (school); an increased awareness of the factors on which his performance is assessed; and an increased ability to monitor his own performance. He has had an opportunity to raise little points which niggle at him, and to ask questions in a free atmosphere. He knows what he can expect by way of training and development in the next year, and he knows that his manager is charged with the responsibility for putting this into practice.

And his manager, at the end of the interview, has a better understanding of the resources available to him. He has thought about the way in which he measures the performance of his people, and that has made him think again about his own job as manager. He has probably learned something about the appraisee which he did not know before. He too has learned something.

The latest report from the Suffolk Education Department (1987) identified listening skills and the ability to direct the course and pace of the interview as the key skills of appraisal interviewing. This document has stressed that the major barrier to communication in an appraisal interview is the conflict in perception between the appraisee's self-image and the image received by the interviewer. The risk of this occurring is much greater when appraisers are evaluating and rehearsing their own answers, rather than *listening* to what the appraisee is saying.

After the interview

One of the most frequently expressed criticisms of appraisal systems is that little is done to follow up issues raised during the interview. It is clearly of vital importance that the appraiser arranges for relevant action to be taken. This may simply be a case of informing others about a particular concern voiced by the appraisee in order that they may act upon it.

Of more significance, is the fact that any subsequent action is unlikely to be taken if the interview was not a valuable experience for both:

> Only if the appraisal interview has been conducted in a very supportive and non-threatening atmosphere can the staff development of which it is a part proceed.

Lusty (1981)

If an appraisal report is to be written, this must be done carefully, honestly and with regard to the discussion held. The appraisee should have the opportunity to amend the report if necessary before it is submitted as an agreed record of the interview.

Summary

This chapter has attempted to spell out, in behavioural terms, the main hallmarks of an interactively skilled person in the context of the teacher appraisal interview. I have tried to demonstrate that real improvement in the skills of appraisal interviewing comes with an awareness of the nature of dyadic interaction as applied to the particular situation of the teacher appraisal interview. To this end I have outlined various appraisal interviewing techniques, emphasising the importance of:

1. adopting a structure or plan for the interview;

2. shaping behaviour so that it influences the appraisee's behaviour to be in step with interview objectives;

3.   probing, reflective and supporting questions.

I have also offered some guidance on pre-interview and post-interview work, and how to manage difficult appraisees.

Finally, much of the guidance given in this article relates to what can be described as 'interviewer style'. The purpose, method and style of the interview should reflect the purpose, method and style of the appraisal system. At Altwood school, the scheme in use is developmental with the emphasis very firmly on self-appraisal through interview. Each school must decide for itself what form it wishes the appraisal system to take. However there can be no doubt that if appraisal interviews are used, the effectiveness and credibility of the scheme will depend largely on the training given in the skills of appraisal interviewing.

4.4 Counselling Skills

Stephen Chelms

Introduction

Appraisal is usually concerned with fixing a value on an object, but when it is used in the context of working with people in a non-profit making situation and in a context of idealism then the conventional formats are not easily applicable. Staff development is a contextual structure in which appraisal, as an annual formal session, in-service training and supervision can be operated. The concern of this brief paper is the skills that can be used both in appraisal and the equally important aspect of follow-up, by a professional tutor, to improve areas after an appraisal interview. Although this paper may be used as a 'reading' or confirmation of what you are already doing or contemplating, it should not be used as a 'manual' to acquire skills. The only way to acquire skills is through a proper system of training.
Much of the material used in this paper is drawn from work in local authority schools, colleges and community education. The people being quoted are professional tutors in training and appraisees themselves. However the examples could apply in a wide range of professions and settings. Quotations are attributed anonymously or to pseudonyms. The paper is in three sections:

1.   The counselling process

2.   A training system

3.   A typology of appraisees

The counselling process

Counselling as an idea and as a profession has really taken off in this country in the last few years. The practice of counselling has entered into many disciplines and institutions in the public, voluntary and private sectors. Counselling covers a wide range of philosophies, techniques and applications. If counselling skills are to be used in appraisal and its follow-up of professional development, then it has to be specific. The whole notion of counselling in appraisal, particularly in education, serves as an *aide-memoire* that appraisal is fundamentally about people. However it is imperative that counselling in this context is facilitative and that it will lead to action. In the organisational structures of education there is insufficient time for long explorations and nor do appraisees, at least ostensibly, come to be counselled. Therefore the appraiser/professional tutor as a counsellor is an educator who needs to complete a task; albeit that the task is centred on people and their careers. The person/career may be inhibited or stagnant, or waiting to take-off. Either way there could be the potential for enhancement. Therefore there are implications to consider about the effect of professional work on personal life and vice versa.

Peter organises courses for community programme workers at a further education college in London. He writes:

> I have an assistant training officer and a departmental assistant working with me. I find the counselling skills I have learned useful in several situations.
>
> Firstly, if I have to formally interview a member of staff about a problem that has arisen, I use my counselling skills to clarify the facts of the situation and find out how that colleague feels about them; I can help them to find an appropriate course of action. Secondly, I find my training helpful in clarifying questions that arise in the course of our work; if I really understand a question I am more likely to make a useful intervention. Thirdly, in monitoring my colleague's work, I find it helpful to be able to assist them to draw up their own lists of what needs doing, rather than give them mine. I have my own ideas and share them as appropriate, but they have the most detailed knowledge of what they are doing; my role is to help them prioritise and evaluate their progress. Finally, I think it is both more human and also conducive to a better working environment if my colleagues feel they can talk to me about personal problems they may have.

Peter's statement is a summary of a curriculum for training in counselling skills and their application. The essential theme is encapsulated in the sentence, 'I use my counselling skills to clarify the facts of the situation and find out how that colleague feels about them; I can help them to find an appropriate course of action'. In using the skills he has learned, Peter is applying a model which is: *the ability to structure a process of clarification, understanding and action*.

The elements are both sequential and in continual use throughout the process. Structuring a process means being able to establish communication, allowing two adults to exchange views at a peer level, with the counsellor having the leading skills. This type of structured communication is essential when you could be overwhelmed by paperwork, by a setting not conducive to counselling, and with a 'client' who is not, in the first instance, present voluntarily, and may perceive the appraiser as an agent of management. Setting the right environment is a skill and in the situation of appraisal the right environment may very well depend on the confidence and concentration of the appraiser.

Clarification is a vital first and continuing activity. It is achieved by listening and mirroring back what has been said, in a type of precis, but only using the words that have been used. This will enable the appraisee to in turn listen to what he or she has been saying in a more objective way. Where a word or a phrase is not clear then the counsellor can, at the right moment ask for clarification, but never at this early stage expand any point or issue. 'It is clearer to me how not to be hung up on the first issue which can sidetrack the interview.' (William, an area community education officer, leading a team of over 20 full-time professional staff.)

Whilst the professional skill at this stage is illustrated, there are also personal abilities. The mirroring back is not to be robotic, it has to be with meaning, because it is not only a sharing of the clarification but also a human communication. The counsellor and the appraisee both have feelings, but in this structure it is important for the counsellor to help without being subjectively involved intellectually or emotionally. The appraisee will, in the course of the process, be enabled to explore, clarify and understand what he or she is saying and feeling, as appropriate to the person and the issue. Appraisees who are dominated by their intellect need to find a balance with their emotions, so they and their work reflect real experience. Those who are dominated by their emotions need to use their intellect to uncover their cognitive abilities. The counsellor has to avoid identification and association with the appraisee and the content of the interview, and at this stage, avoid giving advice. The intervention for clarification has to be natural, when the appraisee finishes a statement or when the counsellor cannot hold any more of the content, intellectually or emotionally.

The measurement of whether the clarification is correct will come from the appraisee, 'that's right!', even though he or she had actually said it in the first place. The mirroring-back will build up a number of points or funnel the content down to a theme or essence. Through this structure the appraisee will 'take the lead', which is a very important development. The appraisee will be owning the content and if they have got what it is, then through greater clarity, they can deal with it. This episode is concluded with a summary which is even more effec-tive and educational if made by the appraisee. The above description is a simplified form of a process which can take place over one or more sessions or occur a number of times within those occasions. This clarification phase is a relearning of basic communication which has been distorted by pressured modern living.

Clarification is in itself a form of understanding but there is a deeper and more precise level which will be essential in the process. This is the **understanding** phase which is the fulcrum of the total process. It is where the negative can be moved to the positive. It is where the themes and issues that have been clarified can be distilled into a 'reading' of the situation. To produce this synthesis needs further concentration by the counsellor. It is an advanced form of active listening, and requires being able to put aside the irrelevant and the 'red herrings' and having a 'helicopter' view of the appraisee's situation, both emotionally and intellectually.

It is preferable for the 'reading' to be a joint effort. We do know who we are and what we wish to do but so often we do not have the mechanism to tap into the accumulation of our personal experiences. It is an educational problem and therefore appraisal and staff development by using this type of counselling structure, can be educative. In the joint effort the counsellor will need, in some degree, to enable the 'reading'.

There has been expression, clarification, response, selectivity and summarising. With both concentration and imagination the appraiser should now be able to feedback a concise picture, of not only what has been expressed but also the appraisee's intellectual and emotional balance. This feedback, if accurate will inevitably lead to and facilitate **action**.

The core of the appraisee's need has now been registered. The counsellor, remembering to retain the basic communication process (mirror-back, summary and synthesis) moves to advice, information and testing; i.e. a resource person. Advice was to be avoided in the early stages but when advice is given through a process of clarification and understanding it becomes more meaningful. An appraiser will need to know the appraisee's specialist area or be sensitised to it. At least the appraiser must be able to work at a higher, abstract level of education. As Peter wrote, 'I have my own ideas and share them as appropriate, but they have the most detailed knowledge of what they are doing, my role is to help them prioritise and evaluate their progress'.

This phase calls for a wide educational and cultural knowledge with the ability for 'reality testing'. This 'testing' takes a suggested course of action and locates it in the reality of the appraisee's personal or professional life as appropriate. The 'testing' of the course of action, which is the solution to the clarified and understood problem, need or issue, can take a number of forms depending on the appraisee and the counsellor's capacity. Review of documentation, role-playing (used selectively and succinctly) of an inter-personal activity, or programme planning are just three of the types of 'testing'.

This counselling approach needs personal and professional training. It is not necessarily a universal solution; it really cannot work with everyone. However, if progress cannot be made directly with the appraisee it does enable, even after only one session, an assessment to be made by the appraiser. Whatever the outcome, systematic training is required to gain the skills and knowledge to conduct the counselling process.

A training system

The particular training system described here is that run by the agency, West Central Counselling and Community Research, of which the author is the executive director. This system is operated through a programme of courses entitled, 'Education for Personal Work'.

The programme teaches the skills and knowledge needed to operate the counselling process described above.

The philosophy and practice of the training comes from a synthesis of; commercial management training, social research, practice and personal development of individual and group therapy and analysis, and especially the concepts and methods of Professor Eugene Heimler, an innovator in therapeutic and education work. Whilst the system is relatively new, Heimler's work has an academic and research basis.

Heimler's interview model and his 'Scale of Social Functioning' are the basis of the system's foundation course. The interview has a definite structure for active listening providing feedback of a concise picture to facilitate action. Whilst the method provides a structure, the advanced practitioner should use it as a seamless process.

The 'Scale' is a set of life questions which cover current satisfactions, frustrations and an overview of the past and future. Examples of these questions are:

Do you like the work you are doing?
Have you a close friend in whom you can confide?
Do you feel your partner understands you?
Is your imagination painful to you?
Do you find that people are unappreciative of your efforts
Do you tend to get over-active or over-excited?
How far has life given you enough scope for self-expression?

These and the other 50 or so questions concretise established psychological insights. The 'Scale' can mathematically score the perceptions of the subject's satisfactions and frustrations and their balance or imbalance. The scale also gives a framework for evaluation and a focus for exploration to be used in a session by the counsellor and the 'client'.

Although it is not always possible to use the 'Scale' directly with a 'client' it does sensitise the counsellor to the complexity of emotional energy. The system teaches a way of working directly with people which involves students in personal development and skills training. This training focuses on the need for the opportunity to speak about the issues which are important to us to someone who has the ability to help us move on to action. Although some people may have the innate qualities to undertake this work, personal and professional skills training develop them in a purposeful way. The system is careful to ensure that the student experiences the process before being taught the skills and informed of the theory. The model is about how to structure a process of clarification, understanding and action.

To be a counsellor demands personal development and professional skills. It also demands direct knowledge of the appraisee's area of expertise or being sensitised to it. An additional body of knowledge is a general understanding of the types of appraisees.

A typology of appraisees

A typology is a useful set of general guidelines. Not everyone fits neatly into a type and there may well be a part of, one or more, types within each of us. There are four types in two groups, and here a fifth has been added.

The first group is where progress can be made, it probably contains the larger number of appraisees. The *ideal* is a person who is clear, has proven abilities, is healthily vulnerable and open to learning. The tutor may have to face the fact that he or she is appraising someone who will become, or is already, more able than him or her. This type therefore will not be content with conventional procedures and will have the abilities of differentiation, overview and synthesis.

The other type in the first group is, at first impression, opposite to the ideal. He or she is not able to express themselves clearly except with words and feelings of frustration. This person is usually *stuck*. They may have been given a job or task which is beyond or not right for them, although they may have made some achievements, even recently. Alternatively or additionally they may have a temporary emotional or domestic problem. This may have been exacerbated by their work problem. The appraisee's manager needs to be realistic about the expectations of delivery and performance. The counsellor may need to arrange a short series of personal consultations, outside of the workplace, for the appraisee so he or she can find expression for the fused personal and professional difficulties. 'I needed to say how I felt and what I can do well, and now my colleagues and team leader are listening to me.' This frustration can be turned round if the feelings are listened to and integrated in clarification with the facts of the work situation.

The second group of types is where progress is difficult and often due to poor management over a period of time. The **obstructive** type comes in a number of forms and those concerned are often talented and intelligent. The 'barrack-room lawyer' who defends other kindred spirits and especially his or her own contract of employment. Another form is the one whose perception of work is decided by the latest 'single issue', e.g. anti-racism and cannot or will not, understand that there could be other causes of social problems besides the one in current vogue. Other forms are avoiding being managed and account- able, and causing inter-personal problems with colleagues.

The obstructive appraisee is a professional management and account- ability problem. Over a period of time an enormous amount of emotional energy and money may have been spent trying to rectify the situation. Inevitably the manager will need to invoke a disciplinary procedure which may rectify the difficulty or lead to its final con- clusion. The professional tutor has a role here, not as a tool of management, but as a clarifier and mediator following appraisal. Attempts to rectify these difficult situations, include managerial super- vision, and tutoring to facilitate a more positive attitude by the appraisee. Even though the chances of success may be limited, it is one of the results of appraisal to make clear to management their responsibility to deal with the problem.

The other type in the second group has a **terminal** problem. The appraisee has been allowed to occupy a post which is unsuitable for him or her. There is no way they can achieve, let alone progress, in their tasks. Even if specialised training is offered it is not taken seriously, 'why do I need training, I can do the job', or, 'I will do the training if you say so'. This is a sad situation because the appraisee often means well, puts in the hours, and genuinely believes that he or she is doing a good job; 'all I need is more time in the day'. The tutor can feel like the doctor who is trying to tell the patient that he or she has a terminal illness, and the patient simultaneously describing his or her long-term plans!

A satisfactory solution to this problem is to move the appraisee across, therefore not losing status, into a larger setting, where he or she will be less likely to make errors. An alternative is help the appraisee explore the possibility of a job within education or outside of it which is more suitable to his or her abilities. These attempts need to be made otherwise the outcome may be a form of dismissal with compensation after a long drawn-out procedure and with the appraisee still not understanding the reasons.

Manifestation of this type may be prevented by sound recruitment and selection of personnel. The 'Peter Principle' should be avoided and staff should not be appointed because there is no one else or they show good will. The selection process needs to be made more professional.

Beyond and within the two groups is the fifth type, the **quintessential**, who can be found, in a limited way, in each of us and sometimes dominates in appraisees. This type may say the right things, may have abilities and may have achieved. Often though there is too large a gap between their self-assessment and their measured and observed abilities. They may talk of wanting to learn more, in fact they talk a lot, but paradoxically for some one typed quintessential it is difficult to get to the essence. They may subscribe to the importance of processes but stop at really being exposed to, or in one. In tutoring these appraisees it is often fruitless to push and confront them very directly with their problem. It is likely to make them more closed and could lead to a trauma or a psychosomatic illness.

All of us at sometime or other feel we are going through chaos and confusion, fortunately it is often brief and we resolve the attendant problem or it is resolved. However there are a few who carry this state for a long time and it could become acute, particularly in mid-life. Unresolved problems from the past will need specialist help and a sound appraisal system will need to be aware of other professional resources.

To work within the system it could be useful to gather a number of observations from those in contact (managers, trainers and acceptable colleagues) with the appraisee. If presented sensitively, but firmly, by the tutor then movement is possible.

Conclusion

This paper has presented a counselling process, a training system and a typology of appraisees. Hopefully this material will help in the consideration of implementing appraisal and its follow-up. Appraisal cannot be an isolated event; an annual session is only effective if it is part of a continuing staff development programme. Such a programme is a form of adult education.

4.5 Training and Preparation Exercises

Alan and Audrey Paisey

Introduction

As with all innovations, the introduction of an appraisal scheme depends upon several critical factors if it is to be carried out successfully. In this case two factors predominate. One is the technical factor, which includes many elements such as having good documentation, the right interviewing skills, sensible procedures and a suitable and acceptable ethical framework. The other and more substantive factor is ideological in nature in that it concerns values and attitudes and may require a shift of ground if appraisal is to become part of normal professional life in teaching.

Training and preparation exercises undoubtedly help to pave the way for the establishment of an effective appraisal scheme in educational institutions. But to date the record of training and preparation initiatives for appraisal is limited. As a contribution to those efforts which are being made, a number of exercises are presented in this chapter. They have all been field-tested and subsequently used in management courses in one context or another. They have been found to be useful but have no prescriptive standing. The ideas in them are capable of varying representation and application according to the needs of those involved and the stage of development of their institution. *They are intended to provoke thought and serve as vehicles for staff discussion and developmental review*.

The introduction of appraisal inevitably requires preparations. These may take the form of:

    (a)   discussions among the staff to understand any scheme which may have to be put into practice ready made or to design and evolve a scheme which is best fitted to the institution's own conditions and needs, if there is discretion to do so; and

(b)   devising procedures and any documents which may be
        necessary for the scheme adopted, testing them out
        experimentally, conducting any modifications required
        and implementing the full scheme.

Exercises which have training potential but can also contribute directly
to the preparations for introducing an appraisal scheme can form a
part of the total programme of preparatory work.

Training activity 1: making a job description

It is impossible to conduct a satisfactory appraisal of a member of staff
without a job description. This, however, need not be written: it might
be tacit. But it is in practice virtually unavoidable to have a written form
of job description at some point or other. Many heads and other staff
profess to having reservations about the usefulness and applicability
of job descriptions in teaching - a few voicing rooted objections. Those
who oppose their use usually base their position on allegations that a
job description is too binding. But in fact *a job description should be
regarded as dynamic, not static, in concept. It may be rewritten
from time to time as jobs develop and as, indeed, job holders
develop*. Written and rewritten job descriptions help the manager to
have an accurate overall picture of the developing organisation.
In this first exercise the objective is to reach agreement about the job of
each member of staff. The exercise consists of three parts with the use
of the simple Job Description Form shown as Figure 8:

1.   A member of staff completes the form in respect of his or her
      own job.

2.   A member of staff completes the form in respect of a colleague's
      job for which he or she has responsibility, e.g. member of
      department or year team.

3.   The two documents are then compared by the two members of
      staff and any anomalies are resolved. Any unresolved matters
      may need to be discussed with the head or other senior staff.

This is an exercise to introduce the idea of job descriptions and their
negotiation. Much work has been done on job descriptions in other
organisations and the interested reader is referred to Ungerson
(1983).

Date Prepared

Name

Position held

Job concerned

  Reports to

  Supervises

Job Authority (i.e. extent of discretion)

Job Content (i.e. actual tasks to be done)

Figure 8 – Simple job description form

Training activity 2: thinking about standards of job performance

The job description is a useful basis for conducting an appraisal, since both the appraiser and the appraisee are at least enabled to talk about the same thing. But to bring some kind of precision into the process there needs to be a reference to **standards**. If standards of job performance are attached to a job, they provide the job holder with something to aim at and those with more senior responsibilities with a measure to offer a fair appraisal.

Towards this end, this second exercise involves taking the completed job description a stage further, using the standards of job performance display shown as Figure 9 - with reference to the definitions contained in Figure 10. The **types of standard** can occur in each of the **categories of standard**, so the idea is to identify a pattern of standards for a particular job by considering each important element of the job and deciding the category and type of standard for each element. Thus one of the cells of the matrix in Figure 9 applies to each important element of the job description. The individual job holder would again play a central part but the head and other senior staff would need to indicate their interests. A series of discussions between individuals and in small groups could be used to accomplish this exercise.

Training activity 3: interviewing and being interviewed for appraisal

Step 1

Divide staff into groups of three. If possible - and numbers allow - group according to compatibility but otherwise put together those who work least closely with one another in the normal working day.

Types of Standard	Contributory	Historical	Comparative
Positive			
Negative			
Zero			

Figure 9 – Standards of job performance display

Types of standard

POSITIVE STANDARD = What we know we want

(Giving clear target of achievement to the job holder)

NEGATIVE STANDARD = What we know we do not want

(Giving maximum area of discretionary action to the job holder)

ZERO STANDARD = What must not happen at all

(Giving minimum area of total constraint to the job holder)

Categories of standard

CONTRIB. STANDARD = Specific contribution of job towards overall objective

(Emphasizes team spirit, sense of responsibility, accountability)

HISTORICAL STANDARD = Continuation or modification of existing standard

(Emphasizes pride in the job, reliability, self-justification)

COMPARATIVE STANDARD = A standard set by reference to performance elsewhere

(Emphasizes competition, market appeal, awareness)

Figure 10 – Reference definitions for exercise 2

Step 2

Brief the trios. In turn each will be an appraisee, an appraiser and an observer. Each trio needs to be in a separate room if possible or at least in different corners of the same room. The observer each time should sit close enough to his or her two colleagues to be able to hear what is said and see the details of the interactions but not close enough to distract attention and be unwittingly drawn into the interview. Allow a *minimum* of 30 minutes for each of the three interview slots. The basis for each is current performance in the job held by the particular interviewee. The first five minutes of each interview slot should be used for the appraisee and appraiser to prepare. The interview itself should last for 20 minutes. The final five minutes can be used by the observer to report his or her findings to the appraisee and appraiser. The observer should focus on the content of the interview and the behaviour of both the appraiser and the appraisee.

Note: The observer may use a simple form to record his or her observations by listing the strengths and improvements needed in the behaviour of the appraiser and the appraisee.

Step 3

In plenary session, each trio reports its general findings to provide a basis for discussions.

Training activity 4: introducing the idea and practice of appraisal

This exercise consists of five linked parts. It offers an opportunity for discussing the idea of appraisal itself as well as the practical and procedural issues which the introduction of an appraisal scheme would entail. Each member of staff completes the five stages of the exercise individually, in pairs or in small groups. Findings may be discussed in groups or by the staff as a whole after all five steps have been completed or at any of the interim stages as thought appropriate. There are no completely right or wrong answers but suggested solutions are offered as shown in Figure 12.

Step 1

The parts and functioning of any system which is established in a school for the purpose of staff appraisal will reflect a balance between the rights and obligations of the teacher as an employee, and those of the head, representing the employer. Rights and obligations in this context are primarily moral and professional in nature rather than legal.

A *right* may be taken as a 'just or legal claim'.

An *obligation* may be taken as a 'moral or legal duty'.

In Figure 11, 40 such rights and obligations are listed in random order. Tick the appropriate box for each according to whether you think an item is

–a right of the employee (REE)
–an obligation of the employee (OEE)
–a right of the employer (RER)
–an obligation of the employer (OER)

In a few cases if you think an item represents two of these equally well, tick both boxes concerned.

An alternative way of carrying out step 1 which may be more appropriate, especially if time is short, is to write out the 40 suggested solutions from Figure 12 and invite participants to tick a box indicating whether they agree or disagree with each of the 40. Points of disagreement can then be discussed.

Step 1   *40 items of Rights and Obligations*

To:		REE	OEE	RER	OER	
1.	assume the individual knows and understands what is required of her/him					1.
2.	decide the ownership and use of written records					2.
3.	accept one's responsibility towards the organisation					3.
4.	have an effective appraisal scheme					4.
5.	make the best use of the time available in appraisal interviews					5.
6.	provide reasonable and proportionate means for professional development					6.
7.	review records fully for interview					7.
8.	be objective and non-abusive					8.
9.	make clear what the minimum performance standards are					9.
10.	hold any written record or reports which are to be kept					10.
11.	be enabled to grow in the job					11.
12.	receive value for money					12.
13.	correct organisational performance					13.
14.	recognize and reward the attainment of required performance					14.
15.	have a clear job description					15.
16.	accept the authenticity of agreed reports and records					16.
17.	receive adequate warning and be subject to proper arrangements					17.
18.	give undivided attention					18.
19.	be appraised					19.
20.	account for one's own performance					20.
21.	be frank on paper or in interview					21.
22.	co-operate in appraisal scheme					22.
23.	be listened to					23.

STAFF APPRAISAL IN SCHOOLS AND COLLEGES

To:		REE	OEE	RER	OER	
24.	expect proportionate consideration and opportunities which are fair to colleagues					24.
25.	expect minimum performance standards to be reached					25.
26.	provide appraisal					26.
27.	be receptive and accommodating					27.
28.	reach and record conclusions on performance					28.
29.	have every help and encouragement to do the job as expected					29.
30.	renegotiate the individual's contribution to the organisation					30.
31.	give reasoned explanations and be able to reply					31.
32.	offer the individual developmental opportunities					32.
33.	provide security for written records					33.
34.	make genuine effort to reach required performance standards					34.
35.	be enabled to make a different contribution to the organisation					35.
36.	provide a non-threatening performance review procedure					36.
37.	give adequate attention to the preparation of documents/interview					37.
38.	have understood the required minimum performance standards					38.
39.	make written records for future reference					39.
40.	have individually negotiated minimum performance standards					40.

Figure 11 – Rights and obligations in appraisal

Step 2

Every right has a matching obligation and vice versa. From the 40 items in step 1 make the best possible 20 matching pairs by entering the item numbers in the table below. There will be 10 such pairs for the employee and 10 for the employer.

EMPLOYEE

Right	Obligation

EMPLOYER

Right	Obligation

Step 3

From step 2, each pair in the employee's table can be linked with a pair from the employer's table to make a set.
Place your choices in the table below and give reasons for them.

	Item Number		Reasons for Choice
	Employee	Employer	
Set A			. . . .
Set B			. . . .
Set C			. . . .
Set D			. . . .
Set E			. . . .
Set F			. . . .
Set G			. . . .
Set H			. . . .
Set I			. . . .
Set J			. . . .

Step 4

Listed below are 10 suggested important elements of an appraisal system. They are in a set order. Place alongside each in the space provided your set from step 3 which best represents it.

Elements	Set	Item Nos.
Organisation Development	. . . .	. . . .
Political Will and Effort	. . . .	. . . .
Accountability	. . . .	. . . .
Minimum Performance Standards	. . . .	. . . .
Appraisal Scheme	. . . .	. . . .
Professional Development	. . . .	. . . .
Preparation for Appraisal	. . . .	. . . .
Conduct of Interview	. . . .	. . . .
Quality of Interview	. . . .	. . . .
Written Records	. . . .	. . . .

Step 5

Use the grid below to indicate how far you think your school or college accepts and understands each of the 10 elements listed in step 4. The grid has space for you to score anything from one to 10 sets on anything from one to 10 levels.

	SET										
	A	B	C	D	E	F	G	H	I	J	
High											1st Level
											2nd Level
											3rd Level
Level of											4th Level
Understanding											5th Level
and											
Acceptance											6th Level
Currently in											7th Level
Your School											8th Level
											9th Level
Low											10th Level

Suggested Solutions Sheet

Step 1

1.	RER	11.	REE	21.	RER	31.	REE
2.	REE	12.	RER	22.	OEE	32.	OER
3.	OEE	13.	OER	23.	REE	33.	OER
4.	OER	14.	OER	24.	OEE	34.	OEE
5.	OEE	15.	REE	25.	RER	35.	REE
6.	RER	16.	OEE	26.	RER	36.	OER
7.	OER	17.	REE	27.	OER	37.	OEE
8.	OEE	18.	OER	28.	RER	38.	OEE
9.	OER	19.	REE	29.	REE	39.	RER
10.	RER	20.	OEE	30.	RER	40.	REE

Step 2

EMPLOYEE		EMPLOYER	
Right	Obligation	Right	Obligation
15	20	1	36
2	16	10	33
35	3	30	13
19	22	26	4
23	5	28	18
11	24	6	32
17	37	39	7
31	8	21	27
40	38	25	9
29	34	12	14

Step 3

As laid out in Step 2 solutions above

Step 4

Elements	Set	Item Nos.
Organisation Development		35,3,30,13
Political Will and Effort		29,34,12,14
Accountability		15,20,1,36
Minimum Performance Standards		40,38,25,9
Appraisal Scheme		19,22,26,4
Professional Development		11,24,6,32
Preparation for Appraisal		17,37,39,7
Conduct of Interview		23,5,28,18
Quality of Interview		31,8,21,27
Written Records		2,16,10,33

Figure 12 – Exercise for introducing the idea and practice of appraisal: suggested solutions

SECTION 5
FORMULATING AN ACTION PLAN

5.1 Formulating an Action Plan

Bob Cooper and Brian Fidler

Introduction

The object of this book has been to discuss a range of issues which it is necessary to consider before an attempt is made to introduce a system of appraisal into a school or college. It has also brought together in the form of six case studies some of the accumulated experience of those who have already travelled some way along the path, and have set up systems of appraisal. The stage has been reached where the formal appraisal of teachers and lecturers is likely to become a statutory requirement, and therefore all educational institutions will have to face a number of these issues if they have not already done so. The nature of the education system in this country at present is such that individual institutions still have a great deal of freedom to initiate systems which, in the professional judgement of the staff, are appropriate for that school or college at this moment in time. How long this state of affairs will last in the face of the centralising control mechanisms which are now being contemplated, we have no means of telling, but because of it there is now a great deal of accumulated wisdom about both the introduction and the ongoing process of appraisal in educational organisations. It is still considerably less than the experience of industry in this regard but it is nevertheless significant. If this knowledge and experience can be shared it will undoubtedly prove to be of value.

This last section attempts to bring together some of the facts and some of the ideas which have been discussed more fully elsewhere. The attempt has been made to put together an action plan, a model which incorporates the stages of an implementation strategy. At each stage the range of possibilities is briefly discussed. Like all models it is inevitably simplified and abbreviated but it is hoped that this will provide a suitable summary and conclusion to this collection.

Climate

The importance of a good general climate of staff relations has been stressed in almost all of the articles in this book. For a staff appraisal scheme to be effective it needs to be set in a climate of mutual trust and confidence. The introduction of an appraisal scheme into a school or college is part of the general management of a developing institution; it should not be something which is merely bolted on in response to external pressures. It will only succeed if it is seen to be an integral part of the existing management practice. Because of this the form and the style of the scheme adopted will vary from one institution to another just as the management and leadership style will inevitably vary from one institution to another. Even if the procedures for appraisal are standardised by a local authority, individual schools and colleges will need to discuss how best to adapt those procedures to fit into the existing management framework. If the general management style is bureaucratic then it will probably be more appropriate to introduce a standardised and rational system. If the management style is more collegial, or what Handy (1985) calls a 'person culture', then the form and the procedures may have a looser, more democratic nature. Whatever form or style is adopted the channels of communication between the senior management and the staff need to be effective. Information needs to be shared and staff need to feel able to discuss the issues freely and openly.

Institutional plans

One of the factors which all the successful organisations investigated by Peters and Waterman (1982) in the USA and Goldsmith and Clutterbuck (1984) in the UK had in common was that they had clear objectives and a shared sense of where the firm was going. Educational institutions need a similar sense of common purpose. Of course the essential purpose of any educational institution is the education of its students, but the way in which that purpose is to be achieved needs to be discussed and agreed by the staff concerned. There needs to be a shared sense of where the institution is going and the means by which the objectives are to be attained. Once some kind of agreement has been reached about objectives then it is possible to discuss ways in which the resources available to the institution can be employed to meet those objectives. This will include looking at the most valuable resources available – namely the human resources. A policy can be agreed about staff development needs in the light of the discussion concerning objectives. The general staff development policy can then be further refined at departmental and sectional level.

All staff development should be seen in the light of both institutional and individual needs. If the institutional policy is agreed first then the necessity for some system to identify individual needs in the light of this policy becomes obvious.

It is also important at this point to fully establish the many constraints which inevitably surround all development activities. All institutions have financial constraints and have to make economic choices. The financial constraints on education at the moment are particularly severe and individual teachers need to be made fully aware of the reality of the situation which individual schools and LEAs have to face. There are also constraints upon the institution in relation to time and the availability of expertise. In an ideal situation the school or college may want to send one of its staff away on a particular course which would be of benefit to both the individual and the institution, but it may not be able to do so because that member of staff's expertise cannot be replaced at this moment. Once a need has been identified it is right that action should be agreed to meet that need, but the action must also take fully into account the various constraints which have to be considered. There is no doubt that the introduction of a staff development and appraisal system generates expectations about in-service opportunities. This indeed is one of its functions. The longer term success of any scheme introduced will depend on how those expectations are fulfilled. Many writers of case studies have spoken of the honeymoon period which occurs at the beginning of a new headship or on the introduction of a new scheme. Nothing can ruin a honeymoon faster than expectations not being realised! If all parties in the appraisal process are aware of the background against which decisions have to be made then it is possible to ensure realistic expectations.

Consultation

Appraisal is an emotive subject for many teachers and lecturers, and everyone needs time to adjust to new ideas and new situations. Means must be found if a new system of appraisal is to be introduced into a school or college to provide opportunities for the staff to talk about the ideas and to discuss their individual concerns and their worries. This cannot always be done in large open meetings, in which many staff are diffident about speaking in front of large numbers of colleagues. The consultative process takes time but there is a large amount of evidence, not least from Japanese industry, to testify to its effectiveness. Part of the process may be to invite visiting speakers who have already introduced a system of appraisal, to talk about their experiences. Another part may be to go through the very necessary preliminary process of job analysis and the development of job descriptions. These activities inevitably involve staff and enable them to feel part of the decision-making and planning procedures.

Planning

Once agreement has been established in principle there are a range of issues which need to be discussed and upon which decisions need to be taken. Many of these issues are discussed more fully in Sections 1, 2 and 4 of this book. For those in colleges, a useful set of discussion papers has been assembled by Field (1987).

It is generally appropriate to establish a working party or a series of working parties with clear terms of reference and with a definite timetable to produce firm recommendations for the staff as a whole. The working parties should have a clear brief to bear in mind all the various resource implications and constraints when they are making their reports.

In particular the costing of the time required for all aspects of the process will need to be given careful attention. This should include any administrative or secretarial requirements in addition to the time of teaching staff.

Some of the issues upon which decisions need to be made are as follows. These are not prioritised in any way. It may also be that some of these decisions may be taken at LEA or DES level.

(i)   *What is the purpose and style of appraisal?*

The three broad aims of appraisal are:

1.   it should carry credibility with the public as a check on the quality of work in schools and colleges;

2.   it should lead to improvements in the learning experiences of pupils and students;

3.   it should lead to greater job satisfaction of all those who work in schools and colleges.

What priority is to be accorded to each of them? On the account-ability-development display on p.3, where should the proposed system be placed? How far should the process be a professional dialogue between peers and how far should it be a dialogue between superior and subordinate or manager and managed? Is an objective of the system really to be the improvement of the performance of every teacher? Answers to these questions will reflect the values of the organisation and the style of management into which the appraisal process must fit. Agreement on these fundamental issues has implications for many of the subsequent more detailed questions.

(ii)   *Who is to be appraised and who is to do the appraisal?*

Decisions will need to be taken about the overall comprehensiveness of the scheme. Will it include every member of staff or will it be voluntary in the first instance? Is there to be superordinate, subordinate or peer group appraisal? Will there be appraisal by grandfather – that is appraisal not by the immediate superior, but by the person one above him or her in the hierarchy? Will there be an appeal to grandfather or to the head? Is the headteacher going to appraise all the staff? Is the head or the principal to be appraised? Is there to be appraisal by line managers? Are the line managers – that is, in general, heads of department – aware that they have that kind of management responsibility? Will the appraisal system include non-teaching staff? How are part-time staff to be fitted in?

(iii)   *Confidentiality*

Decisions will need to be made about the confidentiality of some of the discussions which will take place as part of an appraisal system. An agreed system will need to be worked out concerning the nature of the records themselves, what information is to be written down, where the completed records are to be kept, and who is entitled to see those records. All successful systems of appraisal depend upon the co-oper-ation of staff. If a member of staff is concerned that the things he or she says as part of the appraisal process may be used against them at a later date, there is little chance that there will be a full and frank exchange of views which is the essence of the whole appraisal process.

(iv)   Form of the documentation

There needs to be an agreed job description which includes a statement about standards of performance as a pre requisite to any appraisal interview. There are a number of appraisal schemes where quite deliberately there are no written records kept of the interview. The process in itself is considered to be valuable, and the great difficulty in guaranteeing absolute confidentially it is considered may destroy the open nature of the discussion. The disadvantage is, of course, that if agreements are to be made about targets or goals for development and improvement of performance over a future period, then it is difficult to be precise about what was agreed. It is also much more difficult to effectively monitor progress towards those goals at subsequent interviews. A further point is that no system can ensure that there will be continuity in the pairings of people for the purposes of the interview and if there are no records it means starting from the beginning again with someone new.

In practice most schemes have devised some form of pre-appraisal checklist, together with a form of record of decisions which can be agreed by both parties at the end of the interview.

(v)   Venue and timing

Not least among the decisions which have to be made are those concerning where and at what time of the year the interviews are to take place. In some cases this may be no problem because one person will be doing almost all of the appraising and that person will have an office available which can be used for the purpose. In other cases, where it has been decided that the task of appraising should be spaced among the middle management as well as the senior management, there may well be problems of both time and place which have to be addressed. If heads of department and section heads are to do this as part of their management responsibility, then this needs to be fully acknowledged. Time should specifically be allocated on timetables for this purpose and suitable office accommodation free from interruption by pupils or telephones needs to be found.

Should appraisals be an annual event for all? Or should they be at different frequencies for some? Should there be more than one interview per year? And by different appraisers?

(vi)   *Referral system*

From time to time there will inevitably be differences of opinion about certain aspects of a review. In some cases it may be that the appraisee feels that he or she is being unfairly treated in some way. In other cases the appraiser may feel that he or she is not completely competent to deal with the issues raised. In some cases there may be a genuine clash of personalities which cannot easily be resolved by the two parties concerned. There is a need to establish and to agree some form of referral system through which the two parties, either separately or jointly, may refer certain aspects to a different authority. This is more difficult to arrange if the headteacher is undertaking all of the interviews.

Is there to be a right of appeal against an appraisal report?

(vii)   *Classroom observation*

The issues concerning whether classroom observation should form part of the appraisal process or not will need to be addressed. Interestingly with case studies reported here, only one makes extensive use of systematic classroom observation in the preliminary stages of the process. All the arguments for and against will need to be rehearsed and the various debates about who should conduct the observation, what form it should take and whether any training in observation techniques needs to be given, all need to be discussed. Whatever is decided it is important that as part of the process of appraisal the appraisee should receive adequate feedback about their performance as a teacher from someone who knows the particular context and the special difficulties of that school or college. The object of the whole exercise is the improvement of performance, and one of the best ways of improving one's own performance as a teacher is to receive informed feedback about that performance.

What other forms of data are to be used as the basis for the appraisal interview?

(viii)   *Standards of performance*

Some general guidelines which addressed the notion of expectations of professional standards within the particular school or college would be found very helpful by both appraisers and appraisees alike. These will inevitably reflect the values and approach of the whole organisation. Their articulation will be a very valuable exercise in communication in order to develop further a shared culture within which appraisal is easier to operate.

(ix)   *Outcomes*

What mechanisms are to be used to collate staff development needs identified through appraisal? How are training needs and other developmental opportunities to be co-ordinated across the organisation? How is feedback on individual staff development plans to be given?

What mechanisms are to be used to feed into the management structure organisational problems which are identified as a result of one or more individual appraisals.

What contingency plans should there be to cope with any poor performers who are identified as a result of appraisal? What resources does the school or college have to provide advice, counselling, coaching and support for those who may need them?

Confirming the decision

When the working parties have completed their work there will be a need to share their recommendations with the staff as a whole and to confirm the wish or the requirement to proceed further. It is essential to ensure the commitment of all staff as far as possible, but of the line managers or heads of departments in particular if they are to operate the scheme.

The six case studies (Section 3) in general confirm what has been found elsewhere that, if there has been a full and thorough debate on all the issues, and staff have had opportunities to examine the arguments, there will by that time be a high level of commitment on the part of some staff which will be to some extent counteracted by the mere acceptance of the inevitable on the part of others.

Additionally an opportunity may need to be found for a more wide ranging discussion among the staff as a whole on questions of value and the assumptions behind the management models which are being advocated. These matters are discussed in Sections 1 and 2 and Section 4.1. and 4.2.

Training

The next stage in the process of introduction will be to arrange the form of training. This may take a variety of forms and its extent will vary according to the needs of any particular institution. In addition to training in the essential interpersonal skills which are part of the interview process and which are discussed in Sections 4.2, 4.3, 4.4 and 4.5, there may be a need to consider general management processes in the institution as a whole (see Section 4.2).

Initial training in interview skills, classroom observation skills and other identified skills will be required but there will be ongoing maintenance training required to develop and improve these skills once the appraisal system is working.

If middle managers are to carry out the appraisal of members of their teams and they are to be expected to carry out a greater managerial role, then some consideration should be given to their management training needs as a whole since *an appraisal system is only as good as the managers who have to operate the system*.

Training will not only be required for appraisers but also teachers who are to be appraised. They need to understand the system fully and to have realistic expectations of their role within the process so that they can both contribute and benefit.

Implementation

It is as well to give the people concerned with the interviewing the opportunity to undertake an interview at an early date following the training process. There are often a number of fears and apprehensions which can be overcome through the first real experience of conducting an appraisal interview. One can take part in simulated situations during the training process but it is never quite the same as facing a colleague as part of the real thing.

Monitoring

Following the first interview situation it is often advisable to create the chance for those who have been acting as appraisers to come together to discuss any problems encountered and to assess the experience. This sharing of experience is a further part of the training process and is itself a development activity.

Completion of interviews

The whole process shall now be completed. It is important to try to ensure that all the interviewing is completed by the end of the academic year so that the cycle of appraisal which is of course a continuous one, can have some kind of shape and symmetry.

Allocation of resources

The appraisal interview has a review stage, a diagnostic stage and a commitment to action stage. Having obtained that commitment to action on the part of individual members of staff the school or college as a whole has to find the resources to facilitate that action. How this is done will vary from one institution to another. A number of schools and colleges now have a senior member of staff identified to make these decisions. In smaller institutions it may well be the headteacher who makes the final decision. In some larger schools and colleges there is a staff development committee which has a wide and representative membership, and whose terms of reference are to make recommendations in the light of the institutional plan. However the decisions are made it is important that they are fair and are seen to be fair by staff.

Evaluation

Like other aspects of the work of a school or college the appraisal scheme, once it has been set up and is running, will need to be evaluated. This can either be done through a form of self-evaluation – asking the various participants in the scheme for their views on the process and the outcomes of the system – or alternatively some kind of external audit might be set up. This could take the form of inviting an outside consultant, either a local adviser or inspector or someone from a local college or university to critically evaluate the effectiveness and the efficiency of the whole.

Revision and further training

Whatever form of evaluation is set up the results need to be carefully considered by all those involved in the scheme and then changes made in the light of that evaluation. Teachers are constantly evaluating and appraising the work of their students and attempting to bring about changes in behaviour as a result of that appraisal. On the whole teachers are less good about undertaking systematic evaluation of the school as an organisation and then acting upon the results of that evaluation. Polytechnics and colleges whose courses have been validated by the CNAA are very used to this way of developing courses and have benefited from the process a great deal.

Conclusion

The costs in terms of professional time required to operate an effective appraisal system are high as has been pointed out by Joan Dean earlier in this volume. They cannot adequately be met within present staffing and will require additional funding from central government. This would show a commitment to higher standards in a very positive way.

Like all innovations, appraisal can either be regarded as an opportunity to be seized or as an imposition to be endured. Unless staff appraisal is seized as an opportunity by which the organisation and the individual can both benefit there is a danger that the result will be the imposition of a bureaucratic assessment system which will be inimical to a profession dedicated to development and improvement.

We believe that opportunity is best seized at individual institutional level as part of the management process. As a guiding principle for the implementation of any appraisal system we end with our three overall aims for a staff appraisal system:

1.   it should carry credibility with the public as a check on the quality of work in schools and colleges;

2.   it should lead to improvements in the learning experiences of pupils and students;

3.   it should lead to greater job satisfaction of all those who work in schools and colleges.

Contributors

Stephen Chelms   (Executive Director, West Central Counselling and Community Research, London)

Stephen Chelms qualified at Westhill College, Birmingham, as a youth and community worker, and later at the University of Calgary, Canada, as a lecturer in the Heimler Method of Human Social Functioning. He is currently completing a masters degree on an investigation into professional supervision in the youth service.
West Central is a Jewish foundation which specialises in action-research in the Jewish community and has a training system open to anyone who needs to develop their skills in working with people. It also provides a consultancy service.

Robert Cooper   (Head of Education Management, Crewe and Alsager College of Higher Education)

Bob Cooper trained as a primary teacher and subsequently taught in both primary and secondary schools before being appointed as a lecturer in education at Alsager College. After teaching on initial training courses for some years he is now fully involved in organising and teaching in-service courses in education management, and consultancy work with schools. He is an active member of BEMAS and is currently vice-chair of the north-west branch.

Guy Danhieux   (Vice-Principal(Resources), Swansea College)

Guy was educated at Liverpool and London Universities. He taught for four years in secondary schools and then for seven years in futher education. He has worked in two tertiary colleges. His present responsibilities include being chair of the staff development committee.

Joan Dean   (Chief Inspector, Surrey Education Committee)

Joan Dean has taught at all levels in the education service including a College of Education. She has been headmistress of two primary schools and was for 11 years Senior Primary Adviser for Berkshire. She has been Chief Inspector for Surrey for the past 15 years.

She has lectured widely in this country and abroad and has appeared on radio and television. She has written some 24 books on education, the most recent of which are *Organising Learning in the Primary School Classroom*, *Managing the Secondary School* and *Managing the Primary School*.
She was awarded an OBE in 1980

Peter Delaney   BEd,Dip Man Ed (Headteacher, St Edmunds RC Primary School, Salford)

Head of St Edmunds since 1972. He has contributed at the highest level to a wide range of in-service initiatives related to school management in general and appraisal in particular. His appraisal courses for senior staff in primary school are well established at Manchester University. He has also lectured at conferences and courses organised by the Industrial Society, BEMAS, Manchester Polytechnic and the North West Educational Management Centre at North Cheshire College.

Keith Diffey   BA, MA, MEd (Professional Tutor and Head of the Social Studies Faculty, Altwood C of E Comprehensive School, Maidenhead)

Keith Diffey has been conducting research into the nature of interaction in teacher appraisal interviews since 1984. He is currently studying for a PhD with the Open University.
He has taught in Nigeria and the USA as well as a number of secondary schools in this country.

Brian Fidler   (Head of Administrative Studies Division, Bulmershe College of Higher Education, Reading)
Brian Fidler trained as a teacher and was a lecturer in physics at Huddersfield Polytechnic before undertaking research on the provision of training opportunities in education management at Birmingham University in 1980. At Bulmershe, he has specialised in organising and teaching on training courses in school management. He is secretary of BEMAS Education Management Teachers' Committee.

Joyce Hill   (Headteacher, Irlam Primary School, Salford)

Joyce Hill is in her second primary headship and has been in her present post at a Salford school for three years. Trained at Didsbury

College of Higher Education and the University of Manchester, she is currently completing an MSc in Education Management at Crewe and Alsager College.

John Jennings   (Professional Tutor, Barnet College)

John Jennings has been Professional Tutor at Barnet College in north London for five years. The post being created as part of a new staff development policy. Originally qualified as a chemist, he taught chemistry and mathematics at the college for 15 years. Interests, especially in casework, developed when an ATTI/Natfhe branch officer and liaison committee secretary led to his career change into staff support and staff development.

Alan and Audrey Paisey   (Freelance Consultants in Educational Management)

As freelance consultants in educational management since 1984, Alan and Audrey Paisey have been engaged in designing and running management courses for heads and other senior teaching staff under DES, LEA and private sponsorship. Alan Paisey was previously Head of Administrative Studies and Audrey Paisey the Co-ordinator for Professional Studies in the Junior and Middle School Years at Bulmershe College of Higher Education.

Brian Robinson   (Director of Personnel, Swansea College, Tycoch, Swansea)

Brian Robinson was educated at Middlesex Polytechnic and King's College, London. He studied Geography and Geology. He has had 10 years experience in further education followed by six years in tertiary. As Director of Personnel at Swansea College he has func-tional responsibility for the management of staff development throughout the college.

David Styan   (Headteacher, Marple Ridge High School, Stockport)

David has been head of Marple Ridge High School since 1973. He was a consultant tutor at the North-West Educational Management Centre and has lectured on many courses and at conferences. He was Director of the Centre for the Study of Comprehensive Schools

(CSCS) IN 1984-5 and is a member of the National Council of National Association of Headteachers.

He will take up the post of Director of the North West Educational Management Centre at North Cheshire College, Warrington in April 1988.

Ray Sumner   (Head of External Relations Department, National Foundation for Educational Research in England and Wales)

Ray Sumner taught in England and West Africa before completing a research MEd at Manchester University. Subsequently he worked there in the Education Department on two projects concerned with pupils' characteristics and school performance; at the same time he wrote a PhD thesis on pupils' motivation in school. He was Assistant Regional Director in the North West with the Open University during its first years. He joined the NFER in 1972 to take charge of its guidance and assessment activities. Though retaining an interest in the technical aspects of assessment, he has recently become involved in institutional development as well as undertaking a wide range of consultancy work, mainly for local authorities.

Roy Taylor   (Deputy Headteacher, Altwood C of E Comprehensive School, Maidenhead)

Roy taught in a variety of schools in the north-west and midlands, before coming to his present appointment in 1973, where he has been professional tutor for a number of years and acting headteacher on two occasions.

Staff appraisal formed a major part of his MPhil thesis, 'A Survey and Analysis of Professional Development Practices in the Secondary Schools in one LEA' at Bulmershe College in 1987.

David Trethowan   (Headteacher, Warden Park School, Haywards Heath, West Sussex)

David has been Headteacher of Warden Park School since 1973. He is a cornishman and served for eight years in the Royal Navy before becoming a teacher. His degrees are from Exeter University and his teacher training from Birmingham University, but he says he learned more about staff motivation on a frigate than from any university course. Within seven years of leaving university he was head of a comprehensive school.

David has wide experience of a management approach to schools, developed from long-standing contact with respected industrial and commercial companies. He now teaches part-time on industrial management courses and on headship training courses for LEAs and higher education institutions. David has led, taught or been a trainer on over 100 courses for heads in all parts of Britain. He now runs his own courses in aspects of educational management.

Michael Valleley   (Headteacher, Knutsford County High School, Cheshire)

Michael is a graduate of Leeds University. He taught in Manchester before teaching in three Cheshire comprehensives. He was the head of the art and design faculty and a deputy head before becoming a head. He is a member of the County Commission into Secondary Education and is active in the development of planning and management in education.

John West-Burnham   (Senior Lecturer in Education Management, Crewe and Alsager College of Higher Education)

After 15 years spent teaching in secondary and further education, John West-Burnham now works in in-service education. His main area of interest is personnel management in schools with particular interests in staff development, interpersonal skills and the management of change.

References

Beer, M (1986) 'Performance Appraisal' in Lorsch, JW (Ed) *Handbook of Organizational Behaviour*, Prentice Hall Inc, Englewood Cliffs, NJ (pp.286-300).

Bell, L (1987) 'Appraisal and Schools', in *Management in Education*,1(1), (pp.30-34).

Benderson, AE (1982) 'Teacher Competence', in *Focus 10*, Educ. Testing Service, Princeton, NJ.

BERA (1986) *Appraising Appraisal*, British Educational Research Association, Birmingham.

Blackmer, D, Boysen, V, Brown, C, Pinckney, R, & Walker, RD (1981) School improvement model teacher performance criteria with response modes and standards; a report of the SIM Project, Iowa State University.

Blumberg, A, & Greenfield, W (1980) *The Effective Principal: Perspectives on School Leadership*, Allyn and Bacon, Boston.

Bridges, EM (1986) *The Incompetent Teacher*, Falmer Press, Lewes.

Broadhead, P (1987) 'A Blueprint for the Good Teacher? The HMI/DES Model of Good Primary Practice' in *British Journal of Educational Studies*, XXXV (1) (pp.57-71)

Brown, AF, Rix, AE, & Cholvat, J (1982) 'Changing Promotion Criteria; Cognitive Effects on Administrators' Decisions' in *Journal of Experimental Education*, 52(1) (pp.4-10).

Bunnell, S & Stephens, E (1984) 'Teacher Appraisal: A Democratic Approach' in *School Organization*, 4(4) (pp.291-302).

Cave, R & Cave, J (1985) *Teacher Appraisal and Promotion*, R & J Cave Ltd, Newmarket, Suffolk.

Chapman, W (1983) A context for career decision making, Research Report RR – 88 – 13, Educ. Testing Service, Princeton.

Civil Service (1985) Staff Appraisal: Trainer's Resource Pack, CFL Vision, Gerrards Cross, Bucks.

Darling-Hammond, L, Wise, AE & Pease, SR (1983) 'Teacher Evaluation in the Organisational Context: a Review of the Literature in *Review of Educational Research*, 53(3) (pp.285-328).

Delson-Karan, M (1982) A three-dimensional approach to evaluating teaching performance. Revised version of paper at American Council on the Teaching of Foreign Language annual meeting, New York.

DES (1983) *Teaching Quality*, Cmnd 8836 HMSO, London.

DES (1985) *Quality in Schools: Evaluation and Appraisal*, HMSO, London.

DES (1986) *Better Schools – Evaluation and Appraisal Conference*, HMSO, London.

DES (1987) *School Teachers' Pay and Conditions of Employment: The Government's Proposals*, DES, London.

Diffey, KR (1986) 'Upward Appraisal' in *School Organization*, 6(2) (pp.271-276).

Duigan, PA (1982) 'Developing Behaviourally Achieved Measures of Administrative Effectiveness: Some Problems and Possibilities', *Studies in Educational Administration*, 25.

Everard, KB (1986a) *Developing Management in Schools*, Basil Blackwell, Oxford.

Everard, KB (1986b) 'Staff Appraisal: Lessons from Industry' in *Coombe Lodge Reports*, 18(8) (pp.393-401).

Everard, KB & Morris, G (1985) *Effective School Management*, Harper and Row, London.

Fidler, B (1984) 'Leadership in Post-Compulsory Education' in Harling, P (Ed) *New Directions in Educational Leadership*. The Falmer Press, Lewes

Field, M (1987) 'Preparing for Staff Appraisal' in *Coombe Lodge Reports*, 19(10) (pp.661-689).

Fine, SA (1982) On job analysis and performance assessment. John Hopkins University Symposium on 'Performance Assessment, The State of the Art', (Berk RA) Washington.

Fletcher, C, & Williams, R (1985) *Performance Appraisal and Career Development*, Hutchinson, London.

Fletcher, J (1973) *The Interview at Work*, Duckworth, London.

Freemantle, D (1985) *Superboss: The A-Z of Managing People*, Gower Press, Aldershot.

Fullan, M (1985) 'Change Processes and Strategies at the Local Level' in *Elementary School Journal*, 85(3), (pp.391-421).

Garner, R (1984) 'Restructuring Talks Hit Cash Commitment Snag' in *Times Educational Supplement*, 8.6.84.

Gibboney, R (1987) 'A Critique of Madeline Hunter's Teaching Model from Dewey's Perspective' in *Educational Leadership*, 44(5), (pp.46-50).

Giegold, WC (1978) *Performer Appraisal and the MBO Process: A Self-Instructional Approach*, McGraw Hill Book Co, New York.

Gill, D (1977) *Appraising Performance*, Institue of Personnel Management, London.

Glasman, NS & Paulin, PJ (1982) 'Possible Determinants of Teacher Receptivity to Evaluation' in *Journal of Educational Administration*, XX(2) (pp.140-171).

Glogg, MP (1986) *Examination Results in a Mid-Hants Comprehensive : An Investigation into Management Effectiveness*, unpublished MEd dissertation, Bulmershe College of Higher Education, Reading.

Gray, J (1982) 'Publish and Be Damned? The Problems of Comparing Exam Results in Two Inner London Schools' in *Educational Analysis*, 4(3) (pp.47-56).

Goldsmith, W & Clutterbuck, D (1984) *The Winning Streak*, Penguin, Harmondsworth.

Haefele, D (1981) 'Teacher Interviews' in Millman, J (Ed) *Handbook of Teacher Evaluation*, Sage Publications, London.

Handy, C (1984) *Taken for Granted? Understanding Schools as Organizations*, Longman, London.

Handy, C (1985) *Understanding Organizations*, Penguin, Harmondsworth.

Hawe, M (1987) *The Outward Signs of Inward Grace: The Appraisal of Headteachers in Berkshire*, Bulmershe College Mimeo, Reading.

Hayes, M (1984) 'One Company's Experience with Performance Appraisal' in Kakabadse, A and Mukhi, S (Eds), *The Future of Management Education*, Gower, Aldershot.

Hunter, M (1986) 'Comments on the Napa County, California, Follow-Through Project' in *The Elementary School Journal*, 87(2), (pp.173-180).

Hunter, M (1987) 'Beyond Rereading Dewey: What Next?' in *Educational Leadership*, 44(5), (pp.51-53).

James, CR, & Newman, JC (1985) 'Staff Appraisal Schemes in Comprehensive Schools: A Regional Survey of Current Practice in the South Midlands and the South West of England' in *Educational Management and Administration*, 13(3), (pp.155-164).

James, CR, & Mackenzie, CA (1986) 'Staff Appraisal in the South Midlands and the South West of England – A Survey of Developments During 1985' in *Educational Management and Administration*, 14(3) (pp.197-202).

Jennings, JP, & Skitt, JA (1987) 'Staff Development Handbook' in *Coombe Lodge Reports*, 20 (in press).

Jessup, H & Jessup, G (1975) *Selection and Assessment at Work*, Methuen, London.

Kremer, L, & Ben-Peretz, M (1984) 'Teachers' Self-Evaluation – Concerns and Practices' in *J. Education for Teaching*, 10(1) (pp.53-60).

Laycock, N (1987) 'Appraisal at ICI Plant Protection Division' in **Cooper, R & Fidler, B** (Eds) *Appraisal in Schools and Colleges 'What can be learned?' and 'The Way Forward?'*, Crewe and Alsager College, Alsager.

Leithwood, KA (1982) The principal's role in improving effectiveness: state of the art of research in Canada, paper for International School Improvement Project organised by CERI at Palm Beach; ref.CERI/S1/83.01.

Lloyd, K (1981) 'Quantity Control in the Primary School: the Head's Role in Supervising the Work of Class Teachers' in *School Organisation*, 1(4) (pp.317-329).

Long, P (1986) *Performance Appraisal Revisited*, IPM, London.

Lusty, M (1981) *Staff Appraisal Schemes in Secondary Comprehensive Schools – A Study*, unpublished MSc dissertation, University of Surrey.

McMahon, A, et al. (1984) *Guidelines for Review and Internal Development in Schools(GRIDS): Primary School Handbook; Secondary School Handbook*, Longman, London.

Maier, NRF (1976) *The Appraisal Interview: Three Basic Approaches*, University Associates Inc, La Jolla, California.

Monks, B (1987) 'Appraisal in Further Education' in *Management in Education*, 1(1) (pp.38-41).

Montgomery, D, et al. (1984) *Evaluation and Enhancement of Teaching Performance*, a pilot report (draft), Kingston Polytechnic.

Morrisey, GL (1976) *Management by Objectives and Results in the Public Sector*, Addison-Wesley Publishing Co, Reading, Mass.

Morrisey, GL (1983) *Performance Appraisals in the Public Sector*, Addison-Wesley Publishing Co, Reading, Mass.

Moyles, JR (1987) 'Appraising the Nursery/First School Teacher' in *Management in Education*, 1(1) (pp.35-37).

Murgatroyd, S & Gray, HL (1982) 'Leadership and the Effective School' in *School Organization*, 2(3)(pp.285-295).

Murphy, J, Hallinger, P, & Mitman, A (1983) 'Problems with Research on Educational Leadership: Issues to be Addressed' in *Educational and Policy Analysis*, 5(3) (pp.297-305).

Murray, HG (1983) 'Low Inference Classroom Teaching Behaviours and Student Ratings of College Teaching Effectiveness' in *Journal of Experimental Psychology*. 75(1) (pp.138-149).

NDC (1986) *Appraisal: Annotated Bibliography No.1, 2nd ed*, National Development Centre, Bristol.

NUT (1983) *A Discussion Paper on Formal Teacher Assessment*, National Union of Teachers, London.

Paisey, A (1981) *Organization and Management in Schools*, Longman, London.

Peaker, G (1986) 'Teacher Management and Appraisal in two School Systems in the Southern USA' in *Journal of Education for Teaching*, 12(1) (pp.77-83).

Peters, TJ, & Waterman, RH (1982) *In Search of Excellence*, Harper & Row, New York.

Porter, AC (1986) 'From Research on Teaching to Staff Development: A Difficult Step' in *The Elementary School Journal*, 87(2) (pp.159-164).

Randell, G et al. (1984) *Staff Appraisal*, IPM, London.

Reynolds, D (Ed) (1985) *Studying School Effectiveness*, The Falmer Press, Lewes.

Richardson, W (1987) 'A Perspective from Industry: Industrial Staff Training and Career Development Panacea or Pitfall?' in *School Organization*, 7(1) (pp.13-18).

Robbins, P (1986) 'The Napa-Vacaville Follow-Through Project: Qualitative Outcomes, Related Procedures, and Implications for Practice' in *The Elementary School Journal*, 87(2) (pp.134-157).

Robbins, P, & Wolfe, P (1987) 'Reflections on a Hunter-Based Staff Development Project' in *Educational Leadership*, 44(5) (pp.56-61).

Samuel, G (1982) 'Is the Teacher up to Scratch?' in *Education*, 5.10.82 (p.296).

Samuel, G (1983) 'Evaluation as a Way of Life' in *Education*, 30.9.83 (p.272).

Samuel, G (1984a) 'A Formal Assessment of Performance' in *Education*, 5.10.84 (pp.276-277).

Samuel, G (1984b) 'Towards a Staff Development Review' in *School Organization*, 4(3) (pp.205-210).

Sandbrook, I (1987) 'Appraisal – the System in One Primary School' in Craig, I (Ed) *Primary School Management in Action*, Longman, London.

Schuster, FE & Kindall, AF (1974) 'Management by Objectives – Where We Stand Today' in *Human Resource Management*, 13(1) (pp.8-11).

SHA (1984) *Appraisal of Teachers*, Secondary Heads' Association, London.

Seigel, AI (1982) Work sample and miniature job training and evaluation testing, Johns Hopkins Symposium on 'Performance Assessment, The State of the Art' (Berk RA), Washington.

Sokol, S (1982) Managerial competency, Johns Hopkins Symposium on 'Performance Assessment, The State of the Art' (Berk RA), Washington.

Stallings, J, Robbins, P, Presbrey, L & Scott, J (1986) 'Effects of Instruction Based on the Madeline Hunter Model on Students' Achievements: Findings from a Follow-Through Project' in *The Elementary School Journal*, 86(5) (pp.571-587).

Stallings, J & Krasavanage, EM (1986) 'Program Implementation and Student Achievement in a Four-Year Madeline Hunter Follow-Through Project' in *The Elementary School Journal*, 87(2) (pp.117-138).
Steinmetz, LL (1985) *Managing the Marginal and Unsatisfactory Performer* (Second Ed), Addison Wesley, Reading, Mass.
Stenning, WI & Stenning, R (1984) 'The Assessment of Teacher's Performance: Some Practical Considerations' in *School Organization and Management Abstracts*, 3(2) (pp.77-90).
Stewart, V, & Stewart, A (1977) *Practical Performance Appraisal*, Gower, Aldershot.
Stewart, V, & Stewart, A (1983) *Managing the Poor Performer*, Gower, Aldershot.
Strike, KA & Millman, J (1983) 'Non-Technical Questions About Teacher Evaluation Systems in Elementary and Secondary Schools: A Research Agenda in *Educational Evaluation and Policy Analysis*, 5(4) (pp.389-397).
Suffolk Education Department (1985) *Those Having Torches: Teacher Appraisal: A Study*, Suffolk LEA, Ipswich.
Suffolk Education Department (1987) *In the Light of Torches: Teacher Appraisal: A Further Study*, The Industrial Society, London.
Strauss, GA (1972) 'Management by Objectives: A Critical View' in *Training and Development Journal*, 26(4) (pp.10-15).
Trethowan, DM (1981) 'The Missing Link. Managing the Head' in *The Head*, 1(5) November (pp.22-23).
Trethowan, DM (1983) *Delegation*, Education for Industrial Society, London.
Trethowan, DM (1986) 'Target Setting and Appraisal at Warden Park School' in Day, C & Moore, R (Eds),*Staff Development in the Secondary School*, Croom Helm, London.
Trethowan, DM (1987) *Appraisal and Target Setting: A Handbook for Teacher Development*, Harper and Row, London.
Turner, G & Clift, P (1985) *A First Review and Register of School and College Based Teacher Appraisal Schemes*, Open University School of Education, Milton Keynes.
Ungerson, B (1983) *How to Write a Job Description*, IPM, London.
Weber, R (1978) 'Games Managers Play' in Athos, G, et al, *Interpersonal Behaviour – Communication and Understanding in Relationships*, Prentice Hall, Englewood Cliffs, NJ.
Weirsma, W et al. (1983) Assessment of teacher performance: constructs of teacher competencies based on factor analysis of observational data, American Educational Research Association annual meeting, Quebec.

Whyte, JB (1986) 'Teacher Assessment: A Review of the Perform-ance Appraisal Literature with Special Reference to the Implications for Teacher Appraisal' in *Research Papers in Education*, 1(2) (pp.137-163).
Wood, CJ, & Pohland, PA (1983) 'Teacher Evaluation and the Hand of History"' in *Journal of Educational Administration*, 21(2) (pp.169-181).
Youngman, MB (1983) 'Intrinsic Roles of Secondary School Teach-ers' in *British Journal of Educational Psychology*, 53 (pp.234-243).

Index